Original title: Diving Curiosities. Secrets and Mysteries.

© Diving Curiosities. Secrets and Mysteries, Carlos Martínez Cerdá and Víctor Martínez Cerdá, 2024

Authors: Víctor Martínez Cerdá and Carlos Martínez Cerdá (V&C Brothers)

© Cover and illustrations: V&C Brothers

Layout and design: V&C Brothers

DIVING CURIOSITIES

SECRETS AND MYSTERIES

1

Scuba diving has an ancient history that dates back to prehistoric times.

Large deposits of mollusk shells have been found, many of which live several meters below the sea surface, in the Baltic and along the coasts of Portugal.

These discoveries indicate that primitive humans, unless they waited for significant low tides, had to dive to collect them.

Additionally, in Polynesia, tribes practiced diving from ancient times, using primitive underwater lenses made of a wooden frame holding a transparent sheet of tortoiseshell or sea turtle shell.

The first documented mentions of diving come from 168 B.C., when divers were employed to recover the treasure of Perseus, the last king of Macedonia, who had thrown his palace's treasures into the sea.

In Aristotle's "Problems," two diving devices are mentioned.

The first is the "lebetas," a primitive version of the diving bell, which was an inverted metal container that trapped air inside, allowing divers to descend and reach the seabed from their shelter.

The other device is a breathing tube that resembles the modern snorkel.

In Greek mythology, there are also references to diving.

It is said that a warrior avoided his Persian enemies by breathing through a reed while remaining submerged.

In Persia, divers made goggles from polished tortoise shells, and a legend tells that Alexander the Great used a wooden barrel as a primitive diving bell.

Later, during the Ming dynasty in China, divers transitioned from holding their breath to using a long, curved tube attached to the face with a mask, allowing them to breathe underwater.

Over the centuries, people have practiced free diving to obtain food, sponges, and pearls.

In ancient times, it was common for free divers to reach depths of up to 40 meters (130 feet) without the aid of any breathing equipment.

This practice continues today in many parts of the world, with activities like spearfishing or retrieving objects from the sea floor.

Diving remains a fascinating activity that connects humans with their ancient history and the deep sea.

2

During the Middle Ages, a period generally characterized by a detachment from the sea, the figure of Nicolás, known as "the fish," stands out— a diver whose underwater feats were legendary.

These exploits were immortalized by Friedrich Schiller in his ballad "The Diver" and also appeared as a literary reference in Cervantes' "Don Quixote," where he is mentioned as "Peje Nicolao."

Although this era is not commonly associated with seafaring or marine activities, the existence of Nicolás shows that diving was still a practiced and admired skill at that time.

With the arrival of the Renaissance, an era marked by the rediscovery of knowledge and innovation, diving advanced significantly thanks to the mind of Leonardo da Vinci.

Da Vinci, known for his visionary approach to engineering and design, devised several diving apparatuses.

Among his creations was a simple breathing tube, similar to the modern snorkel, which allowed the diver to breathe while floating on the water's surface.

But Da Vinci's genius did not stop there.

He also designed a full helmet with goggles and an integrated breathing tube, adding a hood with spikes, which is believed to have served as a defense against underwater predators.

Another design depicted a bulky air container that the diver carried on their chest, connected to a mask that covered part of the face.

This device allowed divers to breathe underwater for longer than traditional breath-holding techniques.

Finally, Da Vinci developed an even more complex design, which consisted of a full diving suit, described by some as equipment capable of covering all of a person's vital needs underwater.

This suit was considered an advanced solution for the diving demands of the time, although these designs were not successfully built during his era.

Over the centuries, Da Vinci's ideas influenced the later development of diving, once again demonstrating the Renaissance's ability to reimagine what was possible, even underwater.

3

In the Modern Age, starting in the 18th century, significant advancements in diving technology began to emerge, allowing divers to reach greater depths and stay underwater longer.

One of the first major developments was the appearance and refinement of diving bells.

These primitive structures enabled divers to work underwater while air was supplied from the surface.

Among the earliest versions were the "Patache" by Jean Barrié in 1640, and Edmund Halley's version in 1690, which included a surface air supply system.

Over time, diving bells evolved. One of the most influential figures in this evolution was Augustus Siebe, considered by many to be the "Father of Modern Diving."

In 1837, Siebe revolutionized diving by reducing the size of the diving bell into a helmet that received air from the surface through a pump.

This helmet was complemented by a watertight suit, which kept the diver dry during immersion.

This combination was called the "diving suit," marking the birth of the classic diving equipment.

With some modifications, the diving suit has endured to this day, becoming a symbol of traditional diving.

At the same time, other inventors were seeking lighter and more autonomous solutions.

In 1860, Auguste Denayrouze, a French naval officer, and Benoît Rouquayrol, a mining engineer, joined forces to develop a device that would allow divers greater mobility than the classic diving suit.

This device, called the "Aerophore," consisted of a metal tank containing air at high pressure, between 30 and 40 atmospheres, and was equipped with a regulator and a hose that supplied air from the surface.

What was innovative about the Aerophore was that it allowed the diver to temporarily disconnect from the supply hose and breathe from the air stored in the tank, providing limited autonomy underwater.

However, this device was not widely used because it offered little autonomy and lacked an efficient vision system.

In 1879, Henry Fleuss, a pioneer in the development of autonomous diving equipment, created a device that used oxygen mixtures of 50% to 60%.

This equipment allowed for longer underwater duration and represented a significant advancement in diving technology.

The first dive made with Fleuss's equipment lasted one hour, demonstrating its effectiveness and convincing the London-based company Siebe Gorman & Co. to mass-produce his device.

These advancements laid the foundation for modern diving and marked the beginning of an era in which humans could explore ocean depths with greater safety and efficiency.

4

Yves Paul Gaston Le Prieur (1885 – 1963) was a French Navy officer, a pioneer in the development of autonomous diving equipment, and a prominent figure in multiple disciplines.

Throughout his life, Le Prieur was an adventurer and innovator in various fields.

He was the first man to take off in an airplane from Japanese soil and also the first Frenchman to earn a black belt in judo, highlighting his multifaceted spirit and achievements in both the military and sports arenas.

One of his greatest contributions was the creation of the first self-contained underwater breathing apparatus, now known as S.C.U.B.A. (Self-Contained Underwater Breathing Apparatus).

In 1926, Le Prieur built upon earlier versions of diving equipment but identified a major flaw with existing designs: the dependence on a tube that connected the diver to the surface.

This tube not only limited mobility but also posed a safety hazard.

Le Prieur revolutionized diving by designing a device that allowed humans to breathe underwater without the need for a connecting hose.

His system consisted of a compressed air cylinder and a simple pressure regulator, enabling the diver to breathe directly from the air in the tank.

While this initial equipment did not allow for long dives, it was a crucial advancement that paved the way for future developments in the field of autonomous diving.

Thanks to Le Prieur, for the first time in history, humans could breathe underwater independently, transforming the concept of underwater exploration.

In addition to his innovative breathing apparatus, Le Prieur also developed a full-face mask, a major improvement over the Fernez diving goggles used at the time.

The Fernez goggles were prone to serious issues as divers descended, since the pressure increased and the goggles would press dangerously against the face, causing the dreaded "mask squeeze."

Le Prieur solved this problem by designing a full-face mask that was directly connected to the breathing apparatus.

This allowed the pressure between the mask and the breathing device to remain balanced, enabling divers to descend to greater depths, well beyond the previous limit of 32 feet (10 meters).

Le Prieur's legacy in the development of autonomous diving equipment laid the foundation for subsequent advancements that made modern diving possible.

Although his initial designs did not allow for great underwater autonomy, his work was fundamental to the progress of this discipline, and his vision continues to inspire engineers, scientists, and divers worldwide.

5

Lloyd Bridges was an American actor who gained great popularity for his lead role in the television show "Sea Hunt," which aired from 1958 to 1961.

This show was revolutionary in the way it portrayed the underwater world, introducing millions of people to marine landscapes and the exciting activity of diving.

Bridges played the character of Mike Nelson, a former U.S. Navy sailor turned professional diver, who each week found himself involved in various underwater adventures, from recovering sunken treasures to searching for fallen satellites or solving underwater mysteries.

The series, often narrated from Nelson's perspective, featured the character facing numerous challenges on the ocean floor, surrounded by marine life and exotic creatures.

Through Mike Nelson's exploits, the audience not only experienced the thrill of diving but also discovered the wonders and dangers of the underwater world.

This drew a massive audience that had never before seen the ocean floor depicted so vividly and excitingly on television.

The impact of "Sea Hunt" on popular culture was significant.

The series sparked unprecedented interest in recreational diving and contributed to the boom of diving as a hobby during the 1960s and 1970s.

Many people, inspired by Bridges' character, became interested in exploring the ocean and experiencing for themselves the marine depths that had previously been accessible only to professionals.

Thanks to the series, diving shifted from being an exclusive activity to becoming an accessible and popular practice for the general public.

Lloyd Bridges, who also became an avid diver in real life, was instrumental in this popularization of recreational diving.

"Sea Hunt" played a significant role in creating a new generation of divers and expanding interest in underwater exploration.

Through his performance, the fascination for the oceans and marine life spread, leading thousands of people to enroll in diving courses and embark on underwater adventures.

6

Sylvia Earle, born in 1935, is one of the most important marine biologists in history, as well as an author, explorer, and pioneer in ocean conservation.

Her career spans over six decades of work in the seas, and she has made significant contributions to both marine biology and underwater engineering.

Earle was the first woman to serve as Chief Scientist of the National Oceanic and Atmospheric Administration (NOAA), a key institution in ocean research and protection.

One of the most remarkable milestones in her career came in 1979 when she set the women's depth record by diving to 381 meters (1,250 feet) in a special suit called the Jim Suit during an expedition in Oahu, Hawaii.

This record made her a legend, demonstrating not only her skill as a scientist but also her courage as an explorer.

Alongside her husband, who was a submarine engineer and designer, she developed the Deep Rover, a submersible capable of diving to 1,000 meters (3,300 feet), an unexplored depth at the time.

This advancement in underwater technology was crucial for expanding knowledge about the ocean's deeper zones, enabling research in areas that were previously unreachable.

In addition to her work in underwater engineering, Earle founded Deep Ocean Exploration and Research (DOER), an organization dedicated to creating advanced marine exploration equipment.

Through DOER, innovative technologies have been developed, allowing scientists and explorers to study the oceans beyond what was previously known, contributing to a better understanding of marine ecosystems.

Her work in ocean conservation has been equally influential.

Earle has tirelessly advocated for the need to protect the ocean from both a scientific and ethical perspective, arguing that the planet's future depends on the health of marine ecosystems.

In 1998, Time Magazine named her the first "Hero of the Planet" for her work in marine biology and ocean conservation, an acknowledgment that highlights her global impact.

She has also served as a National Geographic Explorer-in-Residence, where she has been nicknamed "Her Deepness" due to her vast experience and knowledge of the ocean.

Her role at National Geographic has included numerous expeditions and outreach projects that have helped raise awareness among millions of people about the importance of the ocean and the dangers it faces due to human activity.

7

John Cronin (1929-2003) and Ralph Erickson (1922-2006) were the co-founders of the Professional Association of Diving Instructors (PADI), one of the most influential and recognized diving certification organizations in the world.

In 1966, they revolutionized the way diving is taught, making it accessible to a much wider audience by creating a structured certification system that allowed anyone to gradually and safely learn diving skills.

Before the creation of PADI, certifications were more limited, and courses were not as standardized.

Thanks to their vision, millions of people around the world have obtained diving certifications, helping to popularize the sport globally.

PADI, with its focus on safety, education, and accessibility, became a benchmark for diver training and has continued to expand since its founding.

John Cronin, in addition to his crucial role in founding PADI, was a central figure in the diving industry.

He became president of the Diving Equipment Marketing Association and played a key role in expanding this market.

In 1969, he was appointed CEO and president of U.S. Divers, one of the leading diving equipment companies, solidifying his position as an industry leader.

Cronin dedicated nearly 50 years to promoting and growing recreational diving, and his impact on the sport is undeniable.

On the other hand, Ralph Erickson, besides being a co-founder of PADI, had a deep connection with the water from a young age.

After serving in World War II, he founded a swimming school in 1959, reflecting his passion for teaching others aquatic skills.

Erickson was also a pioneer in diving instruction, becoming the 35th instructor in the first instructor class of the National Association of Underwater Instructors (NAUI), another influential organization in the diving world.

Erickson wrote a book titled "Under Pressure," which he used in his classes to teach students about diving.

His ability to effectively and accessibly communicate diving principles allowed him to excel as an instructor.

He was also recognized with numerous awards throughout his life and was inducted into the International Scuba Diving Hall of Fame, a testament to his legacy and contributions to the sport.

Both Cronin and Erickson not only helped popularize recreational diving but also laid the foundations for making diving safer and more standardized, influencing millions of people and the industry globally.

8

Jacques-Yves Cousteau (1910-1997) is synonymous with the history of diving and a key figure in the evolution of underwater exploration.

Co-inventor of the AquaLung, an autonomous air regulator that allowed divers to stay submerged longer and reach greater depths, Cousteau revolutionized modern diving.

His invention marked the beginning of a new era in underwater exploration, enabling scientists and adventurers to delve into the ocean's depths in a way that had never been possible before.

Throughout his life, Cousteau was not only a pioneer in the development of diving equipment but also a tireless advocate for marine conservation and a promoter of the underwater world.

His passion for showcasing the ocean's hidden wonders led him to produce a vast number of documentary films, TV programs, and books.

His work, especially the documentary series "The Undersea World of Jacques Cousteau", gave the general public an intimate view of life underwater, inspiring millions to take an interest in marine ecology and environmental preservation.

During World War II, Cousteau used his knowledge to create, not to destroy.

He formed the French Navy's Underwater Research Group, using the scuba gear he had developed to explore archaeological remains, navigate through minefields, and conduct depth tests.

This group became one of the first underwater research organizations of its time, and their work laid the foundation for many of today's diving techniques.

In 1956, Cousteau designed his own submarine, known as the "diving saucer," which allowed him to descend to a depth of 350 meters.

He used this submersible to film the documentary "The Silent World", which earned him worldwide recognition, including a prestigious award at the Cannes Film Festival.

Later, Cousteau improved his design, creating a version of the submarine capable of descending to 500 meters, further expanding the boundaries of underwater exploration.

His legacy was not limited to diving and filmmaking; Jacques Cousteau was also a fervent advocate for ocean conservation, calling for the protection of marine ecosystems and raising awareness about the dangers of pollution.

He received numerous awards throughout his life, including the Presidential Medal of Freedom, awarded by U.S. President Ronald Reagan.

One of Cousteau's most memorable qualities was his ability to inspire people through his words.

One of his most famous and resonant quotes is: "The sea, once it casts its spell, holds one in its net of wonder forever."

Until the end of his life, Jacques Cousteau continued exploring, teaching, and sharing his knowledge of the sea.

9

Demitri Rebikoff (1921-1997) was an innovative engineer and diving pioneer whose inventions revolutionized underwater photography and both recreational and professional diving.

In 1947, Rebikoff developed the first portable electronic underwater flash, a crucial innovation for underwater photography that enabled divers and explorers to capture images in the dark depths of the ocean.

This advancement facilitated the visual documentation of marine life and underwater landscapes, something that had been extremely limited until then.

Rebikoff also played a fundamental role in the development of underwater vehicles.

In 1952, he created the Torpille, the first underwater scooter, designed to allow divers to move more quickly underwater, saving energy and extending exploration time.

Later, he developed the Pegasus, an improved version of this device.

These innovations transformed divers' mobility and remain an essential part of modern diving equipment.

In addition to his advancements in underwater scooters, Rebikoff continued pushing the boundaries of underwater technology.

He was the creator of the first remotely operated vehicle (ROV), which enabled underwater exploration in places where it was dangerous or impossible to send divers.

ROVs became vital tools for oceanographic research and deep-water exploration, and their impact on the naval industry and scientific research is immeasurable.

Rebikoff was also an active member of the Club Alpin Sous Marin, one of the world's first recreational diving clubs to use autonomous diving suits.

This club, along with other pioneers like Jacques Cousteau, played a key role in developing diving techniques and equipment that are fundamental to modern practice.

Rebikoff designed underwater cameras for Cousteau and other divers of the time, and his collaboration with them contributed to the creation of many tools that made underwater exploration as we know it today possible.

In addition to his technological innovations, Rebikoff was a prolific writer, publishing several books and articles on underwater exploration.

In 1952, he wrote "Exploration Underwater" (Exploration Sous-Marin), a year before Jacques Cousteau released his famous film "The Silent World".

Through his work, Rebikoff contributed to the growing public fascination with diving and marine life, spreading knowledge and techniques that influenced an entire generation of divers and explorers.

Later, Rebikoff moved to the United States, where he worked on various classified projects for the U.S. Navy, solidifying his reputation as a renowned engineer in the field of diving and underwater technology.

10

Boris Porotov, born in Kazakhstan, was a self-taught pioneer of diving in Russia during the 1960s, a time when there was no commercially manufactured equipment or accessible educational material on diving.

He learned the necessary techniques through trial and error, and despite having extremely limited resources, he was able to teach others the practice of diving.

His dedication and perseverance in such a challenging environment made him a key figure in spreading diving in the Soviet Union.

In 1963, Porotov led a group of divers to the Sea of Japan on an expedition that marked the beginning of his legacy in Russian diving.

He returned two years later, in 1965, to produce a film about diving that aired on Soviet television, bringing the underwater world closer to the general Soviet public, who had limited knowledge of what lay beneath the sea's surface.

This film helped popularize diving in the region.

That same year, Porotov established the DIVE diving club, one of the first in Russia.

This club became an important center for the development of recreational and competitive diving in the country and was crucial in training new generations of divers.

Porotov is best known for developing and creating the monofin in 1969.

This invention revolutionized fin swimming and freediving.

The introduction of the monofin to freediving circles in the 1970s led to a series of world records due to the improved performance it offered compared to traditional fins.

The monofin allowed swimmers and divers to move more efficiently and quickly underwater, becoming an essential tool for the sport.

Porotov's skills as an instructor in competitive diving contests were also recognized internationally.

His students broke numerous world records, and his reputation as one of the best diving instructors led to his assignment to train the Soviet Navy's Special Underwater Forces, where his expertise was utilized to enhance military diving capabilities in the country.

Throughout his career, Porotov received numerous awards and recognitions for his work in diving instruction and development.

In 1991, along with his wife, he became an instructor for the Handicapped Scuba Association (HAS), promoting inclusion in the sport of diving.

Together, they opened their own diving school at the port of Sevastopol in the Black Sea, where they continued their work, teaching and training new generations of divers, including those with disabilities, making diving a more accessible activity for everyone.

11

Drowning is a common concern for many people, especially when it comes to water activities like diving.

However, drowning in saltwater, such as in the ocean, is more complicated than most people think due to the properties of the human body and saltwater.

The human body has a lower density than saltwater, meaning it naturally floats.

Saltwater has a higher density than freshwater due to the presence of dissolved minerals and salts, which increases its ability to push objects to the surface.

For a person to drown intentionally or accidentally in the sea, they would have to actively fight against this natural tendency to float.

In activities like scuba diving, it is precisely this buoyancy that can make it difficult for divers to descend efficiently to the seafloor.

That's why divers use weight systems that help them control their buoyancy and submerge safely and in a controlled manner.

These weighting systems allow the diver to counteract the natural buoyancy of their body and equipment, especially in saltwater, enabling them to descend without excessive effort.

The use of an appropriate weight system is essential in diving, as it helps maintain balance and stability underwater.

Divers can adjust the weights they carry based on factors such as the thickness of their wetsuit, the type of water they are in (saltwater or freshwater), and the depth they plan to reach.

Without this system, it would be extremely difficult to control movement underwater and reach the desired depths.

12

Underwater, sounds are perceived very differently from how we experience them on the surface due to the physical properties of water and how they interact with our bodies.

On land, sound travels through the air in waves that reach our ears, causing the eardrum to vibrate, which then transmits the vibrations to the bones of the inner ear, allowing us to interpret the sound.

However, underwater, the process is different, as sound moves through the liquid medium much more efficiently than in the air.

Water is much denser than air, allowing sound waves to travel five times faster.

This means that sounds reach our ears more quickly and are perceived much more immediately.

Moreover, since water is much denser than air, the speed of sound propagation changes, affecting how we perceive it.

Unlike on the surface, sound waves not only reach our ears but also travel through our bodies, which are composed mostly of water (around 65% on average).

As a result, underwater, sounds reach us from different directions simultaneously, making it very difficult to determine where they originate from.

This also affects our ability to locate the source of a sound.

On land, we are very good at locating where a noise is coming from, as we can use the differences in the time it takes for sound to reach each of our ears to determine the direction.

But underwater, sound waves reach both ears almost simultaneously, making it difficult to identify whether a sound is coming from the right, left, or another direction.

Another interesting fact about underwater sounds is that we often only hear the higher frequencies.

This is because low-frequency waves tend to scatter more easily in water, meaning they do not reach our ears as clearly as they do on land.

This contributes to the perception that underwater sounds are strange, distant, or distorted.

This phenomenon can also be a challenge for divers and marine animals, as locating a sound source is much more complicated.

For example, many marine animals, such as dolphins and whales, have developed adaptations to communicate effectively underwater, using specific frequencies and sound patterns that help them overcome some of these limitations.

13

Herbert Nitsch, known as "The Deepest Man in the World," achieved an extraordinary feat by setting the world record for the deepest freedive.

On June 14, 2007, Nitsch reached the astonishing depth of 214 meters (702 feet) in the "No Limits" category of freediving, one of the most extreme forms of the sport.

In this category, divers use a heavy weight to descend quickly and an air-filled balloon to ascend, allowing them to dive deeper than in any other discipline.

This dive took place in Greek waters near the island of Santorini and cemented Nitsch's status as one of the most talented and daring divers in history.

However, this type of dive carries extreme risks.

Although he successfully completed both the descent and ascent, Nitsch suffered severe physical consequences due to the extreme pressure encountered in the ocean's depths.

Upon returning to the surface after the record dive, Nitsch experienced severe decompression, which led to a stroke.

Despite receiving immediate treatment, the aftereffects of the dive impacted his health, and he had to undergo a long recovery.

Fortunately, Nitsch managed to overcome many of the complications, and although he no longer competes at the same level as before, he remains an influential figure in the world of freediving.

Before his impressive 214-meter record, Nitsch had set multiple marks in other freediving disciplines, establishing over 30 world records in various categories throughout his career.

His ability to control his breathing, precise technique, and capacity to remain calm under pressure made him a role model in the sport.

In addition to his "No Limits" record, Nitsch also excelled in other freediving categories, such as "Constant Weight Apnea" and "No-Fins Apnea," where divers must descend and ascend using only the strength of their arms and legs, without the aid of weights or balloons.

Herbert Nitsch is admired not only for his technical and physical achievements but also for his dedication to the science of diving and his commitment to safety in this extreme sport.

14

Rip currents, or undertows, are one of the main dangers for both swimmers and divers.

These currents form when water, after being pushed toward the shore by waves, seeks a way to return to the sea, creating a fast and dangerous flow in the opposite direction.

Rip currents can be so strong that they drag people out to sea within seconds, putting them in grave danger, especially if they are unaware of how to escape them.

For divers, underwater currents, including rip currents, can be difficult to detect from the surface, and once divers are in the water, they can be swept away without realizing the speed or distance they are being carried.

Underwater currents are not always visible, and once a diver is caught in a strong current, swimming against it becomes nearly impossible.

Real-life examples:

 - Accident in the Red Sea: In 2019, a group of experienced divers was exploring a reef in the Red Sea, known for its strong and shifting currents. One of the divers was swept away by an underwater current without realizing it, while the rest of the team tried to descend more slowly. Within minutes, he was carried nearly a kilometer away from the dive site. Fortunately, he had a signaling buoy and was located by the support boat after several hours of searching.

His experience highlighted the importance of carrying additional safety equipment like buoys and whistles for unexpected situations.

 - Cozumel Island, Mexico: In 2016, a diver was caught in a rip current during a night dive at Cozumel Island, a popular diving destination in Mexico. Although the dive began in controlled conditions, a strong current started moving while the group was underwater. The diver was swept out to sea and lost contact with her group. She drifted for over two hours until a local boat rescued her, finding her far from the original dive site. This incident showed how even the most experienced divers can be caught off guard by sudden currents.

 - Great Barrier Reef, Australia: In 2013, a pair of divers got caught in a rip current while exploring a dive site in the Great Barrier Reef. Despite having made a brief dive, both were swept away from their boat. They tried to swim against the current but were unsuccessful. After drifting for hours, they were finally rescued, although one diver suffered severe hypothermia. This case illustrates the danger of attempting to fight a strong current instead of moving parallel to the shore or floating until rescued.

Safety measures:

 - Identifying currents: Before each dive, divers should inform themselves about the local currents and receive a thorough briefing from the dive operator about sea conditions.

 - Safety equipment: It is crucial to carry a signaling buoy (SMB), a flashlight, and a cutting device on every dive.

These items allow boats to quickly locate divers and can help divers free themselves from underwater obstacles.

 - **Swim parallel to the shore:** Instead of trying to fight a current, the safest approach is to swim parallel to the shore to exit the current. Rip currents tend to be narrow and can be avoided this way.

15

The gate syndrome is a phenomenon that divers can experience upon exiting the water, particularly after deep or prolonged dives.

This syndrome refers to sensory overload that occurs when the body and mind face an abrupt change in environmental stimuli when transitioning from an underwater to a terrestrial environment.

The main factors influencing this syndrome are rapid changes in light, temperature, and pressure, which can cause disorientation, fatigue, or even a temporary feeling of disconnection from reality.

When divers are underwater, their senses adapt to low light, cold temperatures, and the absence of terrestrial noise.

The ears perceive sound differently, vision adjusts to lower light, and the body reacts to the water's temperature.

Upon surfacing, the brain must quickly adjust to a completely different environment, which can temporarily overwhelm the senses.

Factors contributing to gate syndrome:

 - Change in lighting: The transition from the dimness of the underwater environment to the brightness of sunlight or artificial light can cause eye strain or momentary visual disorientation. Underwater, light scatters differently, and the eyes become accustomed to a darker environment.

Upon exiting the water, divers may feel momentarily blinded, especially if the sunlight is bright or the artificial light is strong.

 - **Change in temperature:** A diver's body often adjusts to the cooler water temperature. Upon surfacing, where the air temperature may be significantly warmer (or in some cases, colder), the body may experience "thermal shock," affecting physical perception and comfort.

 - **Difference in pressure:** Water exerts constant pressure on the body, and when emerging from this hydrostatic pressure, some divers may feel a sudden release that affects their balance and orientation.
This can contribute to feelings of fatigue or confusion.

Real-life examples and experiences:

 - **Experience in the cold waters of the North Atlantic:** On a diving trip in Iceland, a group of divers experienced gate syndrome after a dive in the Silfra fissure, known for its extremely cold and clear waters. After surfacing and facing the warm air above, many of the divers reported feeling disoriented and exhausted, despite being well-hydrated and having rested before the dive. The abrupt change from water temperature to air temperature caused immediate fatigue. One diver described it as "temporary confusion," as if their body could not properly process the new environment after being submerged in the cold, dark water.

 - **Night dives in the Red Sea:** An experienced diver reported a sensation of sensory overload upon exiting the water after a night dive in the Red Sea. The dive had taken place in complete darkness, with only the light from underwater flashlights to illuminate the surroundings.

Upon exiting the water and removing his mask, he was met by a bright light on the boat, which completely disoriented him. For a few minutes, he felt dizzy and had to adjust his eyes and mind to the reality of the environment. This left him feeling fatigued and experiencing a sense of dissociation, which he directly associated with the abrupt transition from darkness to intense light.

 - **Deep dives in the Caribbean:** A group of recreational divers in the Caribbean reported extreme fatigue after several consecutive deep dives. Upon exiting the water, one of them commented, "I felt like my body completely shut down for a few minutes." Initially, he attributed the fatigue to physical exertion, but later, after discussing it with other experienced divers, he realized that gate syndrome might have played a significant role in the exhaustion. The combination of underwater pressure differences and warm surface temperatures contributed to sensory overload, affecting his cognitive and physical performance for a brief period.

Measures to mitigate the effects:

 - **Gradual transition:** Divers can minimize the effects of gate syndrome by exiting the water slowly, allowing the body and mind to gradually adapt to the new environment. Avoiding sudden changes in light and temperature can also reduce the impact.

 - **Adequate rest:** After a dive, it is important to rest sufficiently before re-entering the water or engaging in any intense physical activity. This helps the body adjust to changes in pressure and temperature.

 - **Hydration:** Dehydration can increase feelings of fatigue and confusion.

Drinking enough water before and after a dive can help prevent these effects.

 - **Use of sunglasses:** To avoid sensory overload caused by the change in lighting, wearing sunglasses or finding a shaded area after exiting the water can protect the eyes and allow them to adjust more gradually.

16

Barodontalgia.

Also known as "pressure-induced tooth pain," this phenomenon occurs in divers when rapid pressure changes during ascent or descent in a dive affect the air cavities within the teeth.

Although it is not very common, it can be extremely painful and, in some cases, can cause dental fillings to break or even result in teeth literally exploding due to the buildup of internal pressure.

Barodontalgia occurs because the air trapped in small cavities within the teeth, such as untreated cavities, defective fillings, or weakened enamel areas, cannot equalize with the external pressure properly.

During a dive, atmospheric pressure increases during descent and decreases during ascent.

If the trapped air within a tooth cannot equalize with the pressure change, it can expand or compress, causing extreme pain.

In severe cases, this can lead to tooth fractures or dislodged fillings.

Teeth in worse condition, such as those with cavities, defective fillings, or incomplete dental work, are particularly susceptible to barodontalgia, as these areas can act as weak points where air becomes trapped.

Real-life examples of barodontalgia:

- Case of an experienced diver in Egypt: A recreational diver undergoing his advanced diving course in the Red Sea experienced sharp pain in his jaw during a deep dive to 30 meters. Although he had dental fillings a few months earlier, it hadn't occurred to him that they could be an issue during his dives. As he descended, he felt increasing pressure in one of his molars. Upon returning to the surface, the pain was so intense that he decided not to dive for the rest of his trip. Back in his home country, he visited a dentist who discovered that the filling had failed, allowing air to be trapped inside the tooth and causing pressure buildup. The diver had to undergo a new dental repair.

- Story of a dive instructor in Thailand: A dive instructor in Thailand shared his experience with barodontalgia after a series of daily dives. He noticed that every time he made deep dives, he felt a sharp pain in one of his front teeth, but the pain would disappear as soon as he surfaced. He assumed it was just a temporary irritation. However, during a particularly deep dive to around 40 meters, the pain became so unbearable that he had to abort the dive. When he visited the dentist, they found that an air bubble had formed in a small cavity in his tooth, and the pressure during the dive had exacerbated the problem. The pressure in that cavity had increased so much that the tooth was on the verge of fracturing. The dentist recommended a dental crown.

- Dental explosion in the Caribbean: A more extreme case involved a diver in the Caribbean who, after a dive to around 25 meters, felt such intense pain that he described it as a "burst" in his mouth.

During ascent, one of his fillings broke due to the pressure buildup in an inadequately treated cavity. The filling was literally ejected from the tooth, and the diver had to be taken immediately to an emergency dentist to treat the fracture and prevent infection.

How to prevent barodontalgia:

To avoid barodontalgia, it is important for divers to take proper care of their dental health before diving. Some recommendations include:

 - **Regular dental check-ups:** It is crucial for divers to undergo regular dental check-ups to detect any potential issues that could cause pain or complications underwater. A dentist can ensure that fillings, crowns, or any other dental restorations are well-sealed and that cavities are fully treated.

 - **Avoid diving with cavities or temporary fillings:** Divers should avoid diving if they have untreated cavities or temporary fillings, as these can allow air to become trapped in the teeth.

 - **Inform the dentist about diving activities:** Divers should ensure their dentists are aware of their underwater activities. This will enable the dentist to use materials and techniques that are more resistant to pressure changes.

17

Dry suits, essential for diving in cold waters, can become dangerous if they are not fitted properly or have damage.

A dry suit is designed to keep the diver insulated from the water, allowing a layer of air around the body to retain heat, which is vital in cold conditions.

However, if the dry suit has issues, such as leaks or valve malfunctions, it can compromise the diver's safety in several ways.

The main risk occurs when the suit fills with water due to improper fit or a tear in the material.

If water enters the suit, the diver's buoyancy changes drastically, potentially leading to a rapid and uncontrolled descent to the bottom.

As water enters, the weight increases, making it harder for the diver to ascend, as they lose control of their buoyancy.

This situation is especially dangerous in deep waters, where the diver must ascend slowly to avoid decompression sickness.

Another common problem involves the inflation and deflation valves.

These valves allow the diver to regulate the amount of air inside the dry suit, which helps maintain neutral buoyancy.

If the inflation valve fails and cannot introduce enough air, or if too much air is introduced, the suit can become dangerous.

Too much trapped air can cause the diver to ascend too quickly, potentially resulting in barotrauma or improper decompression.

On the other hand, if the suit cannot be deflated, the diver may lose control of their ascent, putting their life at risk.

There have been several reported cases of accidents due to dry suit malfunctions.

A typical case involved a diver in Arctic waters who experienced a small tear in their suit, allowing cold water to seep in.

The increase in weight made it impossible for the diver to ascend in a controlled manner, putting them in a critical situation until they were rescued.

Fortunately, the diver survived, but the incident demonstrated how a small tear in a dry suit can lead to a dangerous situation.

Another incident occurred with a diver who, due to a poor fit in their dry suit, experienced "air trapping" in their limbs.

During the descent, the accumulated air in his legs caused him to lose orientation, leaving him in an upside-down position underwater.

Unable to release the trapped air, the diver ascended too quickly, risking barotrauma and serious injuries.

To avoid these risks, it is crucial to perform a thorough check of the suit before each dive.

Divers should ensure there are no leaks, that the valves are functioning properly, and that the suit fits well.

Additionally, receiving proper training in the use of dry suits is essential to prevent incidents.

A diver must know how to control their buoyancy and how to respond in an emergency.

While dry suits are a vital tool for cold-water diving, improper use or neglect in maintenance can turn them into a deadly trap.

It is essential to handle them carefully, conduct regular inspections, and receive adequate training to ensure safety underwater.

18

**Ice diving is one of the most extreme
and fascinating forms of diving,
but also one of the most dangerous.**

This activity is primarily done in lakes, oceans, or rivers covered by a layer of ice.

Divers descend through a hole cut into the icy surface and explore the underwater world in extreme conditions.

The main characteristic of this type of diving is that access to the surface is limited by the ice, which adds a significant risk factor.

One of the greatest concerns in ice diving is losing the exit hole.

Once a diver is under the ice, visibility can be drastically reduced, and without an adequate safety system, it's easy to become disoriented.

If the diver cannot find their way back to the hole, the consequences can be fatal, as there is no possibility of freely ascending to the surface due to the ice barrier.

For this reason, ice diving requires specialized preparation and training.

Divers must be trained in under-ice navigation techniques, handling equipment in cold conditions, and specific safety measures for this environment.

Divers are usually tied to a safety line that extends from the entry hole and is managed by a support team on the surface.

This support team is prepared to help retrieve the diver in case of an emergency or if the diver becomes disoriented.

Communication between the diver and the surface team is crucial.

Specific signals are often used through the safety line to indicate that everything is in order or if assistance is needed.

The surface team can pull on the line to guide the diver back to the hole if necessary.

Diving equipment must also be adapted to extreme cold conditions.

Ice divers use dry suits to protect themselves from the freezing water, which can be close to or even below the freezing point.

Additionally, the diver's regulator must be designed to prevent freezing, as the expelled air in the cold water can freeze the equipment's components.

Another important consideration is dive time.

Diving in cold water increases the risk of hypothermia, even with a dry suit.

Therefore, dives are usually shorter than in other conditions, and divers must be alert for signs of body cooling.

Despite the risks, ice diving is a unique and visually impressive experience.

The water beneath the ice tends to be extremely clear, providing unusual visibility in many dives.

The light penetrating through the ice creates unique patterns and colors, and the marine life in these environments is often completely different from that of warmer waters.

In some regions of the Arctic or Antarctica, ice divers may even encounter seals, penguins, or giant jellyfish.

However, tragic accidents have occurred in ice diving, underscoring the importance of safety and preparation.

A notable case occurred in 2014, when an experienced diver became disoriented under the ice of a lake in Norway and was unable to find the exit hole in time, resulting in his death.

Such incidents have led to an increased focus on safety measures and the need to always have a well-prepared support team.

19

Beards and facial hair can pose a real challenge for divers, as they interfere with the watertight seal of the dive mask.

Facial hair prevents the silicone skirt of the mask from properly adhering to the skin, leading to water leaks.

This can be uncomfortable and even dangerous if the water entering the mask interferes with visibility or causes irritation.

Divers with beards often face this issue, especially those with thick or unruly facial hair in the areas where the mask adheres to the face, such as the mustache or sideburns.

When the mask does not seal properly, water can constantly enter, forcing the diver to clear the mask multiple times during the dive, which is not only annoying but also time-consuming, energy-draining, and can be an unnecessary distraction in situations that require concentration underwater.

To address this problem, some divers choose to shave part of their beard or mustache precisely in the areas where the mask contacts the skin, creating a hair-free area that allows for a more effective seal.

However, not all divers are willing to do this, especially those who prefer to maintain their personal style or are accustomed to their facial hair.

A commonly used alternative is to apply a small amount of

lubricant, such as petroleum jelly or a diver-specific wax, to the areas with facial hair before putting on the mask.

This helps improve the seal and reduce water leakage by creating a barrier that fills the gaps between the mask and the facial hair, although this solution may be temporary and needs to be reapplied if the petroleum jelly or wax dissolves or wears off during the dive.

Another option for divers with beards is to use dive masks specifically designed to fit different facial shapes and better accommodate those with facial hair.

These masks typically have a more flexible silicone skirt with greater adaptability, which improves sealing in difficult areas. However, it's worth noting that even with this type of mask, very thick facial hair can still be an issue.

In more extreme cases, some divers have opted to use a type of equipment called a "full-face mask," which covers the entire face, including the mouth and nose.

These masks are designed to provide a complete seal around the entire face, eliminating the need to worry about facial hair.

This type of mask is commonly used in technical or rescue diving but is also popular among recreational divers seeking a definitive solution to leaks caused by beards.

In any case, it's important for divers to perform a fit test before each dive to ensure their equipment functions properly and that the mask is well-sealed, as a poor seal not only causes discomfort but can also reduce safety during the dive.

20

Underwater fossils have been a source of fascination and surprising discoveries for divers, archaeologists, and geologists alike.

Over the years, fossil remains and ancient artifacts have been found submerged in various parts of the world, revealing important details about human history and the geological evolution of our planet.

These underwater findings, ranging from fossils of prehistoric creatures to sunken ruins and treasures from ancient civilizations, serve as witnesses to changes in sea levels, tectonic movements, and volcanic activity over the millennia.

One of the most famous discoveries took place off the coast of Florida, USA, where divers found fossils of woolly mammoths, megalodon shark teeth, and remains of giant sloths that lived millions of years ago.

These fossils, now displayed in museums, help to better understand what North America's ecosystem was like before the glaciers melted and sea levels rose, covering large areas of land that were once exposed.

Another notable example is found off the coast of Israel, at the underwater archaeological site of Atlit Yam.

This Neolithic settlement, dating back around 9,000 years, was discovered by divers and archaeologists beneath the waters of the Mediterranean.

The remains of dwellings, tools, human skeletons, and even wells have provided a unique insight into life in early agricultural communities.

The site also includes the discovery of human skeletons that suggest the earliest known evidence of tuberculosis in the world.

In 2014, divers off the coast of Madagascar found what is believed to be the treasure of the infamous pirate William Kidd.

On the seafloor, a silver bar weighing over 50 kg was unearthed, believed to be part of a lost hoard.

The discovery not only fascinated historians for its link to 17th-century piracy but also sparked investigations into other possible shipwrecks and sunken treasures in the region.

The Baltic Sea is another area rich in fossils and underwater artifacts.

Due to its cold temperature and low salinity, many organic objects, such as wood and bones, are well preserved in its waters.

Divers in the Baltic have discovered fossil remains of prehistoric whales and giant mammals that inhabited the region during the last Ice Age.

Additionally, sunken ships dating back to the Viking era have been found, providing an invaluable window into the maritime and commercial past of the Scandinavian region.

The Mediterranean Sea, with its long history of human civilization, has been the site of countless treasure and fossil discoveries.

The coasts of Greece, Italy, and Egypt, for example, have revealed remains of shipwrecks from ancient Rome, Greece, and Egypt, including amphorae, gold coins, statues, and temple ruins that were submerged after earthquakes and tsunamis.

One of the most famous discoveries in this area is the Antikythera shipwreck, a Roman ship carrying a series of valuable artifacts, including the "Antikythera Mechanism," a device considered one of the earliest mechanical computers in history.

In Australia, divers have found fossils of prehistoric animals in areas that were once lakes or shorelines submerged by rising sea levels.

In some underwater caves, such as those in the Great Barrier Reef, skeletons of giant marsupials that inhabited the region tens of thousands of years ago have been found.

These discoveries have helped scientists understand the evolution of Australian species and how the region's ecosystems changed over time.

In Indonesia, during a diving expedition near the island of Java, fossil remains of giant turtles dating back over 1.5 million years were discovered.

These fossils, perfectly preserved on the ocean floor, provided scientists with insights into how marine species evolved in the archipelago during the Pleistocene.

One of the most impressive discoveries took place off the coast of England, where divers found fossil remains of prehistoric creatures in what was once a vast plain known as "Doggerland," which connected Great Britain to mainland Europe.

Fossils of mammoths, woolly rhinos, and bison, along with stone tools used by prehistoric humans, have provided valuable insights into life during the Ice Age and how climate and sea level changes affected human populations.

These examples show how diving and underwater exploration have played a crucial role in recovering fossil remains and historical artifacts that would otherwise have remained hidden in the ocean's depths.

Underwater fossils not only provide information about the history of life on Earth but also shed light on human migration patterns, species evolution, and climate changes over time.

21

The Bajau tribe, also known as the "sea nomads," is an indigenous group living in the coastal and maritime regions of Southeast Asia, primarily in the waters of the Philippines, Malaysia, and Indonesia.

They are famous for their exceptional ability to dive to great depths and stay submerged for extended periods, all without using diving equipment or oxygen tanks.

This extraordinary talent has fascinated scientists and led to research into how they have developed these abilities that seem to defy human limits.

The Bajau have lived for centuries in a nomadic lifestyle at sea, relying on diving for their livelihood.

They dive to gather food like shellfish, fish, and sea cucumbers, as well as to collect shells and pearls.

Many of them can dive to depths of over 60 meters and hold their breath for several minutes, an impressive feat for anyone without diving equipment.

What makes the Bajau particularly interesting is that their diving ability is not only due to cultural or technical practice but also to unique physiological adaptations developed over time.

A recent scientific study revealed that the Bajau have undergone genetic adaptations that allow them to dive more effectively than other people.

Researchers found that they have significantly larger spleens than people who do not dive regularly.

The spleen is an organ that plays a key role in the body's response to immersion, as it stores oxygen-rich red blood cells and releases them into the bloodstream when the dive reflex is activated, helping them better withstand the stress of hypoxia (low oxygen levels) during prolonged dives.

Spleen hypertrophy is a genetic adaptation that the Bajau appear to have inherited due to their marine lifestyle.

Another surprising aspect of the Bajau is their ability to adapt to diving from a very young age.

Bajau children start diving in their early years, gradually developing the skill to control their breathing, relax underwater, and withstand pressure changes.

They often use hand-held weights or weighted belts to help them descend faster, allowing them to reach greater depths more easily.

Moreover, since they do not have access to modern diving equipment, they rely on traditional techniques and their natural endurance, making their diving style especially efficient.

A real-life example highlighting the incredible capability of the Bajau is a man named Sulbin, a tribe member studied by scientists and documented by various media outlets.

Sulbin can dive to depths of 65 meters and hold his breath for over five minutes.

During one of his dives, it was observed how he remained calm underwater, spearfishing and gathering shellfish, all while demonstrating a remarkable ability to move fluidly and efficiently under the pressure of the water at those depths.

This type of skill, though incredible, is not uncommon among the Bajau, as their lifestyle has produced generations of experienced divers who rely entirely on the ocean for survival.

Their villages are often built on stilts in shallow waters, or they live in floating houses, reinforcing their connection to the sea.

They spend most of their lives in the water, which has allowed them to develop not only impressive skills but also a deep understanding of the marine environment.

Although today many Bajau face challenges due to modernization and fishing restrictions in their territories, their culture and diving skills remain an integral part of their identity.

Over the years, the Bajau have preserved their traditions and diving methods without the use of modern equipment; instead of commercial dive masks, some Bajau make their own rudimentary masks using simple materials like wood and glass.

They also use traditional spears to fish underwater, demonstrating their skill in both survival and diving.

While many professional divers train for years to achieve similar levels of endurance and depth, the Bajau have developed these abilities as part of their daily lives, enabling them to perform tasks that seem impossible for most people.

22

Lost diver syndrome and thalassophobia are two phenomena that can deeply affect divers, often causing reactions of anxiety, panic, and mental disconnection during dives.

Both fears are linked to the experience of being submerged in the vast and sometimes intimidating underwater world, where conditions are very different from what humans are accustomed to on the surface.

Lost diver syndrome occurs when a diver experiences an irrational and intense fear of being completely alone underwater, even when accompanied by others.

This fear can arise from the sense of isolation that the underwater environment often induces.

In the ocean, visibility conditions can change rapidly.

In clear waters, a diver can see for kilometers, but in many dives, visibility may be limited to just a few meters, creating a sense of disorientation.

This can make the diver feel vulnerable or lost, even when surrounded by dive buddies.

In some cases, the lack of reference points underwater can worsen this feeling.

The diver may lose orientation with respect to the surface, become confused about the direction they are swimming, or even lose track of depth.

In extreme situations, this syndrome can lead to panic attacks, which are dangerous as the diver may act impulsively in an attempt to "escape" the feeling of loneliness.

This has been documented in various dive accident reports, where divers, after feeling this overwhelming anxiety, ascended rapidly, risking their health by skipping necessary decompression stops or exceeding safe ascent speed limits.

A real case occurred in the Red Sea, where an experienced diver accidentally separated from his group during a night dive.

Although he was equipped with a flashlight and had good control of his gear, the fear of loneliness in the oceanic darkness began to affect him mentally.

Despite being trained to stay calm, the diver felt as if the ocean was "swallowing" him and entered a state of panic.

He was eventually rescued without major physical harm, but his experience underscores how lost diver syndrome can affect even the most experienced divers.

On the other hand, thalassophobia, or the irrational fear of the deep ocean, affects some divers in a similar way.

This fear is not only related to loneliness but also to the vastness and the unknown nature of the ocean.

The vastness of the water, the darkness found at great depths, and the lack of visual references can create a sense of extreme vulnerability.

For some, the fear is triggered by the idea that there could be unknown creatures or hidden dangers underwater that they cannot anticipate or see.

This anxiety can intensify when divers find themselves in areas where they cannot see the bottom or in open waters where no land is visible.

Thalassophobia can arise even in divers who did not have this fear before starting their career.

For example, one diver shared his experience during a deep-water dive in the Philippines, where he descended to 40 meters.

Despite being an experienced diver, once he was surrounded by darkness and lost all visual references, he began to feel rising anxiety.

The sensation of "floating in the void" triggered a panic episode, forcing him to shorten the dive.

Although he managed to control his breathing and safely return to the surface, after that day, he developed an aversion to deep and dark dives.

This fear of the unknown in the ocean's depths is more common than many might think.

In some cases, divers have given up open-water diving altogether because of this fear.

The lack of visible structures, such as reefs or underwater walls, can make the diver feel insignificant and exposed.

This can trigger an intense emotional response.

Both fears, lost diver syndrome and thalassophobia, are perfectly understandable when considering how alien the underwater environment can seem.

Unlike the surface, where humans can easily orient themselves and see their surroundings, the ocean is vast, dark, and in many cases, unpredictable.

However, there are ways to mitigate these fears.

Proper training and familiarity with diving conditions can help divers develop self-confidence.

Facing these fears in controlled environments, such as dives in clear water or with good visibility, can reduce anxiety.

23

Diving tank explosions are a real risk that can occur if not properly maintained, and these incidents have been responsible for several fatal accidents throughout the history of diving.

Diving tanks, which contain compressed air or gas mixtures like oxygen or nitrox, are designed to withstand extremely high pressures.

However, if they have mechanical failures, structural damage, or are not regularly inspected and maintained, they can become a serious threat.

Most tank explosions occur due to problems with tank integrity.

These tanks are subjected to internal pressures that can reach up to 200 or 300 bar (around 3000 to 4500 psi), and any defect in their structure could cause an explosion.

The most common causes of such incidents include wear, internal corrosion due to saltwater or moisture entering the tank, as well as impacts or dents that compromise the tank material's strength.

One of the most well-known examples of a diving tank explosion occurred in 2016, when a diver at a dive center in Florida lost his life due to an explosion.

In this case, it was found that the tank had been exposed to poor maintenance, allowing rust to accumulate inside.

The tank had been repeatedly filled without proper inspection, and the internal pressure, combined with the fragility caused by corrosion, was enough to trigger a massive explosion that resulted in the diver's death and serious injuries to several nearby people.

Another common cause of explosions is the mishandling of tanks during transport or storage.

A similar incident occurred at a dive center in Mexico, where a compressed air tank exploded after being accidentally struck by other heavy equipment.

The impact caused a rupture in the tank, releasing pressure catastrophically and generating an explosion that severely damaged the facilities and injured several people with fragments from the tank.

There are also cases where the use of incorrect materials in tank manufacturing has caused explosions.

In the 1990s, a series of tanks made with a defective aluminum alloy failed and caused several fatal accidents.

These tanks had microcracks in the metal, making them vulnerable to structural failure, especially under high pressure.

As a result, many of these defective units were recalled, and stricter regulations were established regarding materials used in the manufacture of diving tanks.

An essential measure to prevent these incidents is to subject tanks to periodic hydrostatic testing, generally recommended every five years, along with annual visual inspections.

Hydrostatic tests verify that the tank can withstand filling pressure, while visual inspections look for signs of corrosion, wear, or physical damage that could compromise its integrity.

Additionally, it is essential to fill tanks only at locations that adhere to strict safety protocols and equipment maintenance standards.

In some cases, explosions have also been caused by the incorrect use of compressors to fill the tanks.

Poorly maintained compressors can introduce oil, moisture, or particles into the tanks, which can corrode the interior or even cause fires when gases combine with flammable substances.

In an incident in Indonesia, a tank exploded during filling because the compressor had contaminated the air with oil, leading to internal combustion and a massive explosion.

For divers, the key to avoiding these risks is to ensure that tanks are well-maintained, always filled at certified dive centers, and that safety protocols are rigorously followed.

Additionally, tanks should not be exposed to extreme heat or cold, as temperature variations can affect internal pressure and compromise equipment safety.

24

Diving with giant squids is a rare and mysterious experience that few divers have encountered, as these animals live in the ocean's depths, typically below 300 meters, where light barely reaches and conditions are extremely challenging for humans.

Giant squids (of the genus Architeuthis) are enigmatic creatures that have been the subject of legends and myths for centuries due to their enormous size and life in the oceanic abysses.

Sightings of these animals are extremely rare, as they only occasionally ascend to more accessible zones or are brought to the surface when injured or dead.

One of the few documented encounters with giant squids occurred in 2006 when a team of Japanese scientists filmed one of these enormous cephalopods in its natural habitat for the first time.

The squid was attracted to a depth of about 900 meters using special lures and underwater cameras.

Although it was not a diver who saw it directly, this event was a milestone in the understanding of giant squids, an animal previously known only from remains found on beaches or accidentally caught in fishing nets.

For divers, the idea of coming face-to-face with a giant squid can be both fascinating and terrifying.

These animals can reach up to 13 meters in length, with long, muscular tentacles covered in sharp suckers.

Divers who have encountered large squids, though not necessarily giants, describe the experience as a mix of awe and fear, given the size and agility of these animals in their natural environment.

A notable example of a terrifying encounter with a giant squid comes from diver Scott Cassell, an underwater explorer and filmmaker who has had multiple encounters with giant squids in his career.

On one occasion, Cassell was diving off the coast of California to film Humboldt squids, a species that can grow up to 2 meters and is known for its aggressive behavior.

During the dive, Cassell was attacked by one of these squids, which dragged him into the depths.

Fortunately, he was able to break free before sustaining serious injuries, but the incident highlights the dangers of interacting with these large predators of the deep.

In some cases, divers operating in areas known to host large squid species, such as off the coasts of Japan or Mexico, have reported encounters with these animals during night dives, when squids ascend to feed near the surface.

Although most of these encounters are brief and non-aggressive, the size and speed of these animals can leave a lasting impression on those who witness them.

One of the greatest risks of diving in areas where giant squids inhabit is the lack of visibility.

At the depths where they are found, natural light does not reach, creating a dark and dangerous environment for divers.

Additionally, giant squids are very fast and agile predators, capable of moving at high speed to capture their prey with their long tentacles.

This can make an encounter completely unexpected and potentially dangerous, as the diver could find themselves in a difficult situation before realizing what is happening.

Despite the dangers, the interest in finding giant squids remains high, not only among scientists but also among the most experienced divers who seek a close encounter with one of the ocean's most mythical creatures.

However, the unpredictable nature of these animals and the difficulty of diving to the depths where they live mean that most giant squid sightings still occur by accident or when the animals are found dead or dying at the surface.

25

Diving in waters contaminated with radiation is an extremely dangerous task, and only a very select group of trained divers have undertaken these dives for scientific, exploratory, or cleanup purposes.

One of the most emblematic cases is Chernobyl, where, after the nuclear disaster in 1986, a group of divers risked their lives to help prevent an even greater catastrophe.

These volunteer divers had to enter the highly radioactive water in the basements of the nuclear plant to drain underground pools that, if not emptied, could have caused a massive steam explosion and released radiation at much more dangerous levels.

The story of these three Chernobyl heroes has become a symbol of sacrifice and bravery.

Engineers Alexei Ananenko, Valeri Bezpalov, and Boris Baranov volunteered to open the gate valves and drain the accumulated water.

Despite the water being highly contaminated with radiation, they succeeded in their mission, preventing what could have been a second devastating explosion.

Diving in such conditions was extremely risky, as the waters were filled with radiation, and the equipment available at the time did not offer complete protection.

Despite rumors of their immediate deaths, in reality, two of the three survived for several years after the mission, although they faced severe health problems as a result of radiation exposure.

In another context, there have also been underwater explorations in areas like Fukushima, Japan, where the 2011 tsunami caused a nuclear plant meltdown.

Scientists and technicians have conducted dives and operations in these zones to assess reactor damage, the impact on the underwater environment, and radiation levels in the surrounding water.

These dives require specialized suits and advanced protective equipment, as the radiation in the water can be absorbed by the divers' bodies and cause irreversible harm.

Diving in radioactive waters not only presents the risk of contamination but also puts divers at risk of developing long-term illnesses, such as cancer.

Although there are strict protocols to minimize radiation exposure, simply coming into contact with contaminated water or sediments can cause damage that may not be detected until years after exposure.

Divers working in these conditions undergo rigorous health checks and have strict limitations on the amount of time they can spend underwater.

In terms of real-life examples, some teams of divers at the Fukushima nuclear plant have conducted controlled dives to recover hazardous materials from the nearby ocean, analyze marine life, and evaluate the levels of contamination dispersed after the accident.

These missions are crucial for determining how radiation has affected the marine ecosystem and whether radiation levels pose a risk to coastal communities.

Despite the dangers of diving in high-radiation areas, these divers have played a vital role in preventing greater disasters and collecting critical scientific data.

However, this work is rarely glamorous, and those involved must accept that, despite all precautions, the risk of health damage is high.

In addition to rescue and disaster mitigation operations, there have also been cases where divers have explored underwater sites abandoned or sealed off after nuclear events.

For example, dives into sunken Soviet nuclear submarines or coastal areas that received radioactive waste during the Cold War have been conducted to assess contamination levels and long-term environmental impact.

These dives are less well-known, but they play an important role in monitoring radiation-affected areas worldwide.

Diving in radioactive waters remains one of the most dangerous underwater tasks, and despite technological advancements in protective equipment, the risks remain extremely high.

26

Underwater, divers often experience a significant alteration in their perception of time due to various factors, which can cause them to completely lose track of how long they have been submerged.

This time distortion is common among both professional and recreational divers and is due to the combination of several sensory elements that change dramatically during a dive.

One of the main factors affecting this perception is the reduction of visual stimuli.

Sunlight decreases significantly as the diver descends deeper, making the environment darker and, in some cases, causing everything around the diver to become monochromatic or dark blue.

Without clear visual references and natural light changing throughout the day, divers may feel as if they are floating in a timeless space, making it difficult for their brain to accurately register the passage of hours or minutes.

The lack of auditory stimuli also plays an important role, as sounds travel faster and can become distorted underwater, but overall, the environment tends to be quite silent, especially at greater depths.

Without hearing familiar sounds from the outside world, like conversations, cars, or birds, divers find themselves in a sort of "acoustic bubble," which can contribute to the sensation that time is slowing down or has stopped altogether.

Breath control is another factor that affects the perception of time.

Divers must maintain controlled, regular breathing to conserve their air supply.

This steady, meditative rhythm of inhaling and exhaling, along with the sensation of weightlessness provided by the water, can make the experience feel hypnotic and contribute to a sense of deep calm.

This mental detachment from the passage of time can be similar to what is experienced during meditation or in flow states, where the mind enters a state of high concentration.

Additionally, pressure underwater can have effects on the body and mind, as at greater depths, ambient pressure increases and can affect the brain function of divers, particularly if they haven't properly acclimatized or haven't managed the use of gas mixtures in their tanks.

At extreme depths, some divers experience what is known as nitrogen narcosis, a condition that can impair judgment and cause a feeling of euphoria or even disorientation, further altering the perception of time.

For divers engaged in prolonged dives, such as those practicing technical or cave diving, this loss of time awareness can have safety implications.

An error in estimating how long they have been underwater can lead to exceeding no-decompression limits, increasing the risk of developing pressure-related illnesses, such as decompression sickness.

That's why these divers must rely entirely on their measuring equipment, such as dive watches or dive computers, to monitor the actual time they've been submerged.

A notable example is William Trubridge, a famous freediver who has set several world records.

Trubridge has mentioned in interviews how freediving to great depths can cause time to distort in an almost magical way.

During his multi-minute dives, his mind enters such a deep state of concentration that, upon surfacing, he often finds it hard to believe he spent so much time underwater.

This disconnection from time is partly what allows him to stay calm and avoid panic during his record dives.

Another example is divers who explore underwater caves, such as members of the Hoyo Negro Cave Underwater Exploration Project in Mexico.

In cave dives, where the environment is even more claustrophobic and dark, divers report that the lack of light and repetitive conditions can make them feel as if they've been underwater for just a few minutes, when in reality, they've been submerged for hours.

Careful planning and the use of dive computers are crucial in this type of dive.

27

Emergency ascent.

It is a critical maneuver that divers must perform when facing situations where they run out of air or experience serious technical problems during a dive.

While it is a life-saving technique, performing it incorrectly can result in serious consequences, such as decompression sickness (also known as "the bends") or even arterial gas embolism.

An emergency ascent is performed when a diver cannot return to the surface in a controlled manner, usually occurring when the air supply runs out or there is equipment failure.

In an ideal situation, the diver would ascend slowly, making decompression stops if necessary, to allow the dissolved nitrogen in their body to be released safely.

However, in an emergency, the diver may be forced to ascend quickly, which involves considerable risk.

The most commonly used emergency ascent is the "Controlled Emergency Swimming Ascent" (CESA).

In this type of ascent, the diver swims to the surface while continuously exhaling to prevent the air in their lungs from expanding dangerously due to the decreasing pressure.

This type of ascent is necessary when there is no immediate access to an alternative air source, such as a dive buddy or a backup regulator.

One of the main threats during an emergency ascent is gas expansion in the lungs, as water pressure decreases as the diver ascends and the air in their lungs expands.

If the diver does not continuously exhale, the air can expand to the point of causing lung overexpansion, potentially leading to alveolar rupture or even arterial gas embolism—a life-threatening condition in which air bubbles enter the bloodstream.

Another significant risk is decompression sickness.

During a dive, nitrogen dissolves into the body tissues due to pressure.

If the ascent is too rapid, the nitrogen does not have enough time to be released slowly and form small, safe bubbles that are expelled through breathing.

Instead, large bubbles can form in the blood and tissues, causing symptoms ranging from joint pain to paralysis and, in severe cases, death.

A real example of a poorly executed emergency ascent occurred in Thailand, where a diver, running out of air at a significant depth, ascended rapidly without exhaling.

Although he reached the surface, the diver suffered an arterial gas embolism and, despite treatment in a hyperbaric chamber, experienced permanent neurological damage.

On the other hand, there are cases of well-executed emergency ascents that have saved lives.

In 2018, a diver in the Cayman Islands had to perform a CESA from a depth of 30 meters after his regulator failed.

The diver remained calm, continuously exhaled, and ascended in a controlled manner to the surface.

Although he could not complete a decompression stop, he showed no signs of decompression sickness because he ascended at an appropriate speed and was able to reach the hyperbaric chamber for preventive treatment.

Divers should always train for controlled emergency ascents and practice proper safety techniques.

In diving classes, divers are taught to control their breathing and avoid panic—two crucial factors in an emergency situation.

One of the key principles is that, while the situation may seem desperate, the residual air supply in the lungs is often enough to reach the surface safely if a slow, continuous ascent is performed.

The use of a dive buddy is also essential.

In many emergencies, the buddy can provide an alternative air source, such as a secondary regulator, allowing for a more controlled and safer ascent.

There are numerous cases where teamwork and proper preparation have enabled divers to share air and perform emergency ascents without incident.

28

Dolphins are known for their intelligence, sociability, and communication skills, and there are numerous accounts of surprising interactions between them and humans, especially divers.

In several cases, dolphins have been reported to "rescue" divers in dangerous situations, either by helping them reach the surface or by protecting them from threats like sharks.

A famous example occurred in 2004, when a group of swimmers off the coast of New Zealand was surrounded by a pod of dolphins that kept them together for over 30 minutes.

During that time, the swimmers were unaware that the dolphins were protecting them from a great white shark that was lurking nearby.

The dolphins seemed to sense the danger and instinctively acted to keep the humans safe until the shark moved away.

Another notable case happened in 2013, when a diver named Yang Yun, who was participating in an ice diving competition in China, suffered temporary paralysis due to the cold water temperature.

As she struggled to swim to the surface, it was a beluga whale, a cetacean closely related to dolphins, that gently pushed her upward, saving her life.

This event was widely covered by the media, highlighting the cetaceans' ability to interact with humans in an instinctive and empathetic manner.

Dolphins have also shown protective behaviors in other situations.

In 2012, a group of divers witnessed a dolphin repeatedly approaching them and behaving unusually.

After following it, they discovered that one member of the group was trapped in a fishing net.

The dolphin apparently noticed the situation and alerted the others to help.

In addition to their ability to interact with humans, dolphins have a highly developed sense of communication and environmental perception, using echolocation to detect objects and living beings in the water, even at great distances.

This skill can help them identify dangerous situations before humans can.

Their ability to emit high-frequency sounds, such as whistles and clicks, allows them to coordinate as a group and act quickly, which may have been key in many reported rescues.

While these stories are exceptional, they highlight the unique relationship between dolphins and humans.

However, science has not been able to definitively determine whether dolphins act out of empathy, protective instinct, or simple curiosity, but it is clear that these cetaceans possess remarkable intelligence that allows them to perform seemingly altruistic actions.

In mythology and history, dolphins have been depicted as saviors of sailors and travelers in danger at sea.

29

Diving, while fascinating and full of underwater adventures, can have negative effects on the skin and hair if proper precautions aren't taken.

Prolonged exposure to saltwater is one of the most common factors contributing to accelerated skin aging in divers.

Saltwater tends to dehydrate the skin, stripping away natural oils that help keep it moisturized and soft.

Without proper hydration before and after dives, the skin can become dry, rough, and show signs of premature aging, such as fine lines and wrinkles.

This is worsened if the diver spends a lot of time in the sun, as UV rays combined with saltwater dryness further accelerate skin damage.

Frequent divers often take preventive measures to avoid these issues.

For example, applying a water-resistant moisturizer before diving or using products that create a protective barrier over the skin.

Post-dive lotions or gels containing aloe vera or ingredients that help restore skin hydration are also important.

Hair, in turn, suffers considerably from contact with saltwater or chlorinated pools.

The salt from the sea or chlorine from pools strips the hair of its natural oils, making it brittle, dry, and prone to breakage.

Frequent divers often wear diving caps or apply protective oils to their hair to minimize damage.

Coconut oil or argan oil are popular among divers, as they act as a barrier between the hair and the water, preventing salt or chlorine from penetrating the hair follicle.

Some people even opt for deep conditioning treatments after their dives to restore hair softness and strength.

A lesser-known but potentially harmful effect of diving is the impact of pressure on the skin.

At great depths, water pressure increases significantly, which can cause small areas of bruising on the skin, especially in areas where the wetsuit doesn't fit properly or where the equipment exerts pressure.

These bruises, while generally not dangerous, can be bothersome and indicate that the diving gear is not fitting correctly.

It is essential to wear a properly fitting wetsuit to prevent these pressure-related injuries.

There are reports of divers experiencing skin problems, ranging from rashes to more severe conditions like "diver's skin," where the skin shows signs of long-term damage due to constant exposure to water and pressure.

In extreme cases, divers exposed to high pressure for prolonged periods have experienced damage to the capillaries in the skin, causing visible marks or discoloration.

This phenomenon has been observed in some commercial or technical divers who spend extended periods underwater, sometimes in extreme conditions.

On the other hand, pressure can also affect exposed or poorly protected areas of the body, causing discomfort.

More experienced divers are usually very aware of how pressure impacts not only their ears and lungs but also their skin and body in general.

Properly adjusting the wetsuit and ensuring that contact areas with the diving gear are well protected are essential practices to prevent more serious issues.

30

Diving on a full stomach is something experts advise against due to the effects of underwater pressure on the human body, especially on the digestive system.

As a diver descends, the ambient pressure increases significantly with depth, which can affect the normal functioning of the stomach and intestines.

The additional pressure compresses the gases in the body, including those present in the digestive system, which can create a feeling of discomfort or unease.

One of the most common effects divers experience when diving on a full stomach is bloating or abdominal distension.

As the gas in the stomach compresses and then expands during ascent, divers may feel pressure or abdominal pain.

This phenomenon is more noticeable if the diver has eaten a large meal before the dive, making the stomach feel full and uncomfortable.

Additionally, digestion is a process that requires energy and blood flow, which can interfere with the diver's physical performance underwater.

In some cases, the combination of pressure, movement in the water, and having eaten can cause nausea or vomiting during the dive.

Although vomiting underwater is relatively rare, some divers have reported experiencing it, especially if they suffer from motion sickness or have overeaten before the dive.

Vomiting underwater can be dangerous, as the diver must ensure that the regulator mouthpiece stays in place to avoid the risk of inhaling water.

Dive instructors often train divers to handle this situation by keeping the regulator in their mouth and breathing gently to avoid choking or inhaling water.

Additionally, the digestive system can be affected by the increase of gases in the gastrointestinal tract.

Gases, which normally expand and contract according to the pressure they are subjected to, can cause discomfort in the intestines, leading to flatulence or pain.

In extreme cases, pressure can worsen pre-existing conditions such as gastroesophageal reflux, causing stomach acid to rise into the esophagus, which is extremely uncomfortable and can increase the risk of vomiting.

There are examples of divers who have experienced these effects.

One case documented by a recreational diver involved feeling extremely dizzy and nauseous after a dive in which he had overeaten shortly before descending.

He reported that he began to experience stomach cramps during the dive and had to cut his bottom time short due to the discomfort.

Although he didn't vomit, the experience was enough to remind him of the importance of controlling what he eats before diving.

In a more professional setting, some commercial or technical divers have shared experiences of dealing with stomach discomfort caused by pressure when performing prolonged dives or at greater depths.

The conditions they dive in, with rapid pressure changes, can exacerbate the effects on the digestive system, which is why they tend to be more cautious with their pre-dive meals.

31

Diving in volcanic areas is a unique yet challenging experience, as it involves exploring regions where geothermal activity has a direct impact on the underwater environment.

In certain parts of the world, such as Indonesia, Iceland, and other volcanically active regions, it is possible to dive in proximity to underwater volcanoes or hydrothermal zones.

These areas offer unique underwater landscapes, such as hydrothermal vents and gas bubbles escaping from the seafloor, creating an almost surreal atmosphere.

One of the biggest challenges of diving in volcanic areas is the water temperature.

In certain locations, like the Banda Sea in Indonesia, the waters can be extremely hot due to nearby volcanic activity, reaching dangerously high temperatures in specific areas.

Divers must have specialized equipment, such as wetsuits or drysuits designed to withstand elevated temperatures and prevent serious burns.

The water surrounding underwater volcanoes can be rich in minerals and acids, which can be corrosive to diving equipment if not handled properly.

A famous diving destination in volcanic areas is Sangeang Island, Indonesia, where divers can swim in waters that are in constant contact with volcanic activity.

The island itself is an active volcano, and in the nearby underwater area, you can see gas bubbling from the seafloor.

As you approach certain areas, the water temperature increases significantly, requiring careful attention to avoid heat-related injuries.

In this zone, colorful deposits of sulfur and mineral formations create a unique appearance in the underwater landscape.

Another iconic destination is the region around the island of Santorini in Greece.

Santorini is known for its volcanic history, and beneath its waters lie several volcanic sites where the water is heated due to underwater fumaroles.

Divers can experience gas bubbles emanating from fissures in the seafloor, creating a dynamic landscape and an unusual geothermal environment.

Although the temperatures are not as extreme as in other locations, local guides often recommend appropriate suits and precautions to avoid potential burns.

Diving near underwater volcanoes also carries other risks.

Emissions of gases such as carbon dioxide and hydrogen sulfide can affect visibility underwater and, in some cases, even pose a health risk if gas levels are too high.

Additionally, volcanic activity can generate unexpected currents or alter the underwater landscape unpredictably, requiring divers to have a good level of experience and training.

A notable example of diving in extreme volcanic waters occurred at White Island in New Zealand, which is a partially submerged active volcano.

In 2019, an eruption on the island while tourists were present highlighted the dangers of these active volcanic areas, resulting in a tragic toll of victims due to toxic gases and pyroclastic flows.

Although this incident did not involve divers, it underscores the inherent risk of engaging in recreational activities near active volcanoes, as eruptions can be unpredictable and deadly.

In Iceland, the Silfra fissure in Thingvellir National Park, while not directly volcanic, offers a unique diving experience between the tectonic plates of Eurasia and North America.

Although the water temperature is extremely cold due to the glacial origins of the water, this volcanic area is one of the most geologically impressive and provides a unique experience for divers wishing to explore fissures and geological formations.

32

Weight loss during prolonged diving is a common phenomenon due to various factors that interact to cause the body to burn a considerable amount of calories.

Long dives, especially in cold waters, require greater physical exertion and lead to increased calorie loss, which can result in rapid weight loss if not managed properly.

One of the main factors contributing to weight loss is thermoregulation.

Underwater, the body loses heat much faster than in air, up to 25 times more quickly in cold water.

Although divers use neoprene wetsuits or drysuits to maintain body temperature, the body still works hard to generate heat and compensate for the loss of calories.

This effort to maintain warmth in cold waters can result in significant calorie expenditure.

Diving in colder waters causes the body to burn more calories to stay warm, which can lead to weight loss if energy reserves are not replenished with calorie-dense foods after the dive.

The physical effort associated with diving is also another important factor.

Although it is often perceived as a relaxing sport, diving involves constant muscular effort, both while swimming and while controlling the equipment and managing underwater currents.

Maintaining balance and buoyancy in the water, along with performing tasks such as swimming against currents or maneuvering at different depths, increases energy expenditure.

Even in calm dives, the water's resistance to body movement forces the muscles to work harder than at the surface, accelerating calorie burning.

During prolonged dives, divers may also experience a decrease in appetite due to the pressure underwater.

This can lead to an underestimation of the amount of food needed to maintain adequate energy levels, exacerbating weight loss over time.

For this reason, it is important for divers—especially those participating in prolonged dives or multi-day expeditions—to consume sufficient calorie-rich foods and carbohydrates to offset energy expenditure.

Energy snacks and meals high in carbohydrates are often recommended by dive instructors to ensure that energy levels are maintained during and after the dive.

A real example of this phenomenon has been observed in divers participating in prolonged scientific expeditions or underwater search and rescue operations, where long dives in cold waters are common.

In a documented case in the Arctic, a team of scientific divers conducting dives to study sea ice reported significant weight loss after a week of daily dives.

Despite being equipped with drysuits, divers noticed that their metabolism accelerated due to the low temperatures and constant physical exertion, leading to a loss of several kilograms in just a few days.

Another relevant factor is dehydration, which can also contribute to weight loss during diving.

Despite being surrounded by water, divers can become dehydrated quickly due to breathing through the regulator, which dries out the airways.

Additionally, the compressed air they breathe contains less moisture than ambient air, resulting in greater fluid loss.

Dehydration not only affects physical performance but can also contribute to weight loss if not adequately compensated with fluid intake before and after the dive.

33

Diving has proven to be an effective therapy for war veterans, particularly those suffering from post-traumatic stress disorder (PTSD) and physical injuries.

This therapy, known as "therapeutic diving," combines the psychological and physical benefits of diving in an environment that promotes calmness, relaxation, and rehabilitation.

Immersion in water, weightlessness, and the serene environment contribute to stress reduction, improved physical mobility, and provide a safe space for veterans to confront the emotional challenges they may have faced due to their combat experiences.

One of the key aspects that makes diving such an effective therapeutic tool is the sensation of weightlessness underwater.

For veterans suffering from physical injuries, the feeling of buoyancy relieves pressure on the joints and muscles, allowing them to move with greater freedom and less pain.

This is especially beneficial for those who have suffered amputations or injuries that limit their mobility on land.

In the water, they can perform movements that would otherwise be difficult or impossible, strengthening their bodies and boosting their confidence in their physical abilities.

Programs like "Diving With a Purpose" and "Mission Therapy" have pioneered the use of diving as a form of physical therapy.

On the mental aspect, the underwater environment provides a calm and distraction-free atmosphere, allowing veterans to focus on their breathing and relax.

This can have a profound effect on reducing symptoms of anxiety, insomnia, and stress that often accompany PTSD.

Underwater, veterans do not have to worry about loud noises or stimuli that trigger traumatic memories, allowing them to disconnect from everyday stress and find a space of mental peace.

Diving also promotes mindfulness, as divers must concentrate on their breathing, their equipment, and their immediate surroundings, helping to reduce anxiety and fostering greater awareness of the present moment.

Several studies have documented the positive effects of therapeutic diving on veterans with PTSD.

A study from Johns Hopkins University showed that veterans who participated in therapeutic diving programs experienced significant improvements in their stress levels and emotional well-being.

Another study in the UK also revealed that veterans who engaged in diving reported a reduction in symptoms of depression and anxiety.

In many cases, diving has been used as a complementary therapy alongside other approaches, such as cognitive-behavioral therapy and psychological counseling, reinforcing its long-term benefits.

A real example of the effectiveness of therapeutic diving is the case of a U.S. Navy veteran, Jordan B.

Jordan was diagnosed with PTSD after serving in several combat zones.

Although he received traditional psychological treatment, he still struggled to manage his anxiety and suffered from recurrent nightmares.

Jordan decided to join a therapeutic diving program, and after several dives, he began to notice an improvement in his mental state.

The tranquil ocean environment and the concentration required for diving helped calm his mind and reduce stress symptoms.

After completing the program, Jordan stated that diving had restored a sense of control over his life, something he hadn't experienced in years.

In addition to its therapeutic benefits, diving also provides an opportunity for veterans to rebuild the camaraderie they had during their service.

Often, these diving programs are conducted in groups, allowing veterans to share experiences and support others who have gone through similar circumstances.

This reinforces social bonds and provides a sense of community and mutual support, which is essential for their recovery.

Dive instructors and fellow veterans can also act as mentors, helping to create a support network that extends beyond the therapeutic environment.

The success of diving as therapy for veterans has led to the creation of organizations and programs dedicated exclusively to offering this form of rehabilitation.

A notable example is "Operation Blue Freedom," a nonprofit organization that offers diving programs for wounded veterans.

These programs not only focus on physical rehabilitation but also use diving to restore confidence, mental well-being, and a sense of purpose among veterans.

The success of such programs has demonstrated that therapeutic diving can be a powerful tool in helping veterans overcome the effects of PTSD and physical injuries, providing a new way of healing through water.

34

The phenomenon of divers losing consciousness during ascent, especially in deep freediving, is known as hypoxia syncope or fainting.

This occurs when oxygen levels in the body drop drastically during ascent, leading to a sudden loss of consciousness.

This issue is exacerbated when divers practice freediving at extreme depths, where their bodies do not receive the necessary oxygen to maintain normal brain function.

It poses a significant risk for freedivers, especially those attempting to break depth records or who remain underwater for extended periods.

During freediving, the body is subjected to different levels of pressure that affect the amount of available oxygen.

As the diver descends, the pressure increases, and the air in the lungs compresses.

While the amount of oxygen does not change, the increased pressure facilitates the dissolution of gases such as oxygen into the blood, which can create a false sense of security during the dive.

However, as the ascent begins, the pressure decreases rapidly, and the available oxygen in the lungs drops drastically.

This change can cause blood oxygen levels to fall below what the brain needs, resulting in a loss of consciousness before reaching the surface.

This phenomenon is particularly dangerous because it can occur without warning.

Divers may feel perfectly fine during the ascent, but just before reaching the surface, the brain can run out of oxygen, causing the diver to lose consciousness.

Without immediate support, a diver who faints underwater risks drowning.

For this reason, it is crucial that freedivers always have safety equipment or companions who can intervene quickly if a syncope occurs.

A well-known case of such an incident involved diver Nicholas Mevoli, an American freediver who died during a competition in the Bahamas in 2013.

Mevoli was attempting to reach a depth of 72 meters in a no-fins category.

Although he successfully reached the desired depth and began his ascent, he showed signs of difficulty as he approached the surface.

When he finally emerged, he lost consciousness, and despite immediate rescue efforts, he could not be revived.

His death highlighted the inherent dangers of freediving and the importance of having proper support and constant monitoring.

Another example is the case of French freediver Loïc Leferme, who was one of the most respected freedivers in the world.

Leferme died in 2007 during deep freediving training.

Although he was an experienced freediver and had set several world records, he suffered a syncope during his ascent.

Even though his support team tried to assist him quickly, it was not possible to save him.

This case emphasized that even the most experienced divers are not exempt from the dangers associated with loss of consciousness during ascent.

Such incidents have led to greater awareness of safety in freediving and have driven changes in safety regulations.

In freediving competitions, it is now mandatory to have safety divers prepared to intervene in case a competitor suffers a syncope.

These safety divers must be ready to bring the diver to the surface, remove their nose clips, and ensure they receive oxygen quickly.

Additionally, competition organizers often have medical personnel on-site to respond to emergencies.

One of the preventive measures that freedivers often take is to avoid hyperventilating before a dive.

While hyperventilating can increase the ability to hold one's breath, it also reduces carbon dioxide levels in the body, delaying the feeling of the need to breathe.

This can lead to the diver not realizing that their oxygen levels are dangerously low, increasing the risk of fainting during ascent.

35

Underwater auroras.

It is a unique experience that occurs in polar regions, such as the Arctic and Antarctica, where the northern lights (aurora borealis in the northern hemisphere) and southern lights (aurora australis in the southern hemisphere) create light displays visible from the surface of the water and also below it.

These phenomena result from solar particles interacting with the Earth's atmosphere, generating waves of light projected into the sky.

In polar regions, where divers often explore beneath the ice, it is possible to observe these flashes of light filtering through the ice layers while underwater.

Although the ice acts as a filter, it allows some of the aurora's light to pass through, creating a diffused lighting effect in the water.

Divers describe the experience as magical and hypnotic, as the green, purple, and reddish hues of the auroras dance on the surface and cast shadows in the underwater environment, enveloping divers in a completely unique visual spectacle.

Diving under the ice, especially in extreme conditions like these, requires thorough preparation.

Dry suits are essential to protect divers from the extremely low water temperatures, which are often near or below 0°C.

Extreme conditions in polar regions also add an extra difficulty to the experience, as visibility can be limited and navigation under the ice can be dangerous if proper protocols are not followed.

Divers exploring these areas must be anchored to a safety line that connects them to the exit hole on the surface to avoid getting lost under the ice.

A real example of diving under the northern lights occurred in Norway, where a group of divers explored the icy waters of the Arctic and witnessed how the light from the auroras filtered through the ice, creating a spectacular environment of colors reflected in the ice crystals underwater.

The divers described the experience as surreal, as it seemed that the lights from the sky also came to life underwater, interacting with the underwater landscape and creating an ethereal atmosphere.

Exploring underwater auroras remains rare, as only a few specialized divers venture into these inhospitable areas under such extreme conditions.

However, for those who experience it, it is an adventure that combines the majesty of ice diving with one of the planet's most impressive natural phenomena.

36

Diving with orcas is one of the most exciting and unique experiences a diver can have.

In regions like Norway, New Zealand, and Canada, it is possible to dive alongside these impressive marine animals.

Despite their nickname "killer whales," orcas typically do not pose a danger to humans in their natural habitat.

They are highly intelligent predators, and although they hunt cooperatively, incidents of wild orcas attacking people are rarely recorded.

Orcas actually belong to the dolphin family and are known for their curious and sometimes playful behavior.

In some areas, especially in Norway, divers and underwater photographers dive with them to observe their behavior in the wild.

Norway is particularly famous for orca sightings during the herring migration season when orcas hunt in large groups, offering divers the opportunity to be close to these magnificent creatures.

It is important to remember that while orcas do not pose a direct threat to humans, respect for their space and wild nature should always be maintained.

Divers interacting with them must be careful and follow the guidance of experienced guides to avoid disturbing their behavior.

Orcas are very social animals and may approach divers out of curiosity, but it is always essential not to invade their territory or provoke unwanted interactions.

In the waters of Tromsø, Norway, divers swim alongside these marine predators during the herring migration.

They describe how orcas sometimes approach slowly, displaying peaceful behavior and observing humans with interest.

At other times, the orcas pass quickly while hunting, ignoring the divers and focusing on their prey.

Diving with orcas is an experience that heavily depends on environmental conditions and the behavior of the animals, so it is not always predictable.

However, those who have had the opportunity to dive with these impressive animals describe the experience as profoundly exhilarating, being face-to-face with one of the ocean's most powerful and graceful predators.

37

Immersion diuresis is a curious phenomenon that affects many divers when they are underwater.

This process occurs due to the changes in pressure and temperature that the body experiences during immersion.

When a diver submerges, the body undergoes a redistribution of bodily fluids.

Underwater, hydrostatic pressure compresses blood vessels in the extremities, causing blood volume to shift toward the torso and heart.

This increase in volume in the central part of the body is perceived by receptors in the heart, which in turn send signals to the brain to eliminate excess fluid through urine, leading to the frequent need to urinate.

Another factor contributing to diuresis is immersion in cold water, as the body reacts to the cold by constricting peripheral blood vessels, which also redistributes blood flow toward the torso.

This, combined with pressure, amplifies the effect and results in increased urine production.

Although immersion diuresis is a natural and harmless phenomenon, divers should be aware of dehydration, as the increased urine production can reduce fluid levels in the body.

It is advisable to stay properly hydrated before and after diving to avoid issues related to dehydration, which can affect performance and safety during diving.

38

Giant kelp forests, especially those formed by the algae known as "Macrocystis pyrifera", are among the most fascinating and unique underwater ecosystems that divers can explore.

These underwater forests are primarily found in temperate waters, such as the coasts of California, Chile, Australia, and South Africa, where conditions are perfect for the growth of these enormous algae.

Macrocystis is a species that can reach heights of up to 45 meters, making them as imposing as trees in a terrestrial forest.

The experience of diving in a kelp forest is comparable to walking through a woodland, with the long algae extending toward the surface, creating an environment reminiscent of an underwater cathedral.

Sunlight filters through the canopy of kelp, casting shadows and creating a constantly moving light show.

These forests are crucial habitats for a wide variety of marine life.

Fish, crustaceans, mollusks, and marine mammals like sea otters find refuge and food among the kelp.

Diving in these forests is a unique experience not only because of the biodiversity they harbor but also due to the sensation of being in a place completely different from the usual seafloor.

Divers often find themselves swimming among the swaying kelp, creating the sensation of floating among giant trees underwater.

Conditions can vary depending on the current, as the giant kelp can move significantly, but it is generally a calm environment teeming with life.

In addition to their beauty, these forests play a vital role in the marine ecosystem, as they help absorb carbon dioxide and provide oxygen.

Diving in a kelp forest allows divers to immerse themselves not only in a dreamlike underwater world but also in an ecologically crucial environment.

These types of dives can be conducted at various points along the coast of California, where they have become one of the main attractions for divers.

Locations like Catalina Island are very popular destinations due to the clarity of their waters and the abundant marine life.

The protection of these ecosystems is essential, as giant kelp is vulnerable to climate change and human activity, highlighting the importance of responsible and sustainable diving practices.

39

Deep diving has a significant effect on human physiology, especially in the blood and how the body handles oxygen.

During a deep dive, the increase in pressure in the underwater environment triggers a series of adaptive responses in the body, one of the most notable being the modification of red blood cells.

When a diver descends to great depths, environmental pressure increases significantly, prompting the body to adapt to better manage the available oxygen.

One of these changes occurs in red blood cells, which slightly alter their shape and behavior, allowing for greater capacity to transport and utilize oxygen.

This phenomenon is part of what is known as the "diving reflex," a physiological response that helps the body conserve oxygen during a prolonged dive.

Deep diving significantly affects human physiology, particularly the blood and how the body handles oxygen.

When a diver descends to great depths, environmental pressure increases, prompting the body to adapt and manage available oxygen more effectively.

In turn, the spleen releases more red blood cells into the bloodstream, increasing the oxygen-carrying capacity.

Additionally, the phenomenon known as "peripheral vasoconstriction" reduces blood flow to the extremities, minimizing oxygen consumption in the muscles of the arms and legs, allowing for greater conservation of oxygen for crucial organs.

This is especially useful for freedivers, who can reach extreme depths without using breathing equipment.

This change in red blood cells and the efficiency of oxygen management are essential for enabling divers to withstand the pressure and physical demands of a deep dive, maintaining an adequate supply of oxygen in conditions that would otherwise jeopardize their well-being.

However, it is important to note that prolonged or repeated exposure to great depths can increase the risk of developing dangerous conditions such as nitrogen narcosis or decompression sickness, underscoring the need for proper training and adherence to safety protocols in deep diving.

40

Diving in historical locations is a unique experience that combines underwater adventure with archaeological discovery.

One of the most fascinating destinations for this type of exploration is the submerged city of Thonis-Heracleion in Egypt.

This ancient city, which was an important port and trade center at the mouth of the Nile River, was submerged underwater over a thousand years ago due to a series of natural disasters, such as earthquakes and floods.

Thonis-Heracleion, rediscovered in 2000, offers divers the opportunity to explore an incredibly well-preserved archaeological site.

Underwater, divers can find colossal statues, sphinxes, remnants of temples, and structures from the pharaonic and Greco-Roman periods.

Additionally, hundreds of artifacts such as coins, jewelry, and pottery have been recovered, shedding light on life and trade in this lost city.

Diving in these ruins is a captivating experience, as it allows you to interact with history in a deep and tangible way.

The relatively calm and clear waters of the Egyptian Mediterranean provide good visibility, making it easier to explore these ancient monuments that remain beneath the waves.

Other submerged historical sites include the city of Pavlopetri in Greece, which is considered the oldest submerged city in the world, with structures dating back over 5,000 years.

In Italy, the city of Baiae, famous for its Roman baths and villas, also offers an impressive diving site, with mosaics, statues, and submerged streets that have remained underwater for centuries.

Diving in these locations not only provides an exciting adventure but also allows divers to witness firsthand the interaction between humans and the sea throughout history.

These underwater explorations reveal not only the physical remains of ancient civilizations but also provide a unique insight into how natural disasters and changes in sea level have shaped our history.

41

Countries with the most diving enthusiasts.

- **Australia:** Home to the famous Great Barrier Reef, it has approximately 3 million diving enthusiasts. Its vast coastline and marine biodiversity make it a key location for this activity.

- **United States:** With around 2.5 million certified divers, the U.S. is a major diving hub, with locations like Florida, California, and Hawaii attracting both local and international divers.

- **Egypt:** About 1 million people dive in Egypt, thanks to the Red Sea, which is one of the most spectacular diving destinations in the world.

- **Thailand:** With its tropical islands and crystal-clear waters, Thailand attracts around 800,000 divers, both local and foreign, who explore spots like Koh Tao and the Similan Islands.

- **Maldives:** Known for its coral reefs and marine life, the Maldives receives approximately 600,000 diving enthusiasts each year, most of whom are tourists.

- **Philippines:** Attracts around 500,000 divers, drawn by the diversity of marine life and the accessibility of dive sites like Apo Reef and Tubbataha.

- **Mexico:** With iconic spots like Cozumel, Isla Mujeres, and the Yucatán cenotes, Mexico has about 400,000 diving enthusiasts who enjoy its tropical waters and underwater caves.

- Indonesia: With its thousands of islands and marine biodiversity, it has around 350,000 enthusiasts, attracted by places like Raja Ampat and Komodo.

 - France: It has approximately 300,000 diving enthusiasts, with locations such as the French Riviera and Corsica, as well as underwater historical sites.

 - Japan: It has a diving community of about 250,000, with Okinawa being one of the main destinations due to its warm waters and coral reefs.

42

Superstitions of famous divers.

 - Herbert Nitsch: The renowned freediver who set depth records has a superstition of not discussing the dive beforehand. He believes that talking about the details before the dive brings bad luck.

 - Enzo Maiorca: This legendary Italian freediver always wore the same lucky necklace that his mother had given him before each dive. He considered this item as protection during his deep dives.

 - Audrey Mestre: The famous freediver who tragically lost her life during a world record attempt always wore a bracelet given to her by her husband, Francisco "Pipín" Ferreras. She never dove without it.

 - Gérard Huet: This French diver always did a shallow dive the night before a major exploration. He believed this "blessed" the dive and gave him peace of mind before facing a bigger challenge.

 - Natalia Molchanova: The most successful freediver in history followed a strict ritual of meditation and breathing before each dive to ensure her mind was clear and focused.

 - Jacques Mayol: Famous for being the first man to surpass 100 meters in freediving, Mayol believed that connecting with dolphins during his training brought him luck and protection. He always tried to interact with these animals before a major dive.

- **William Trubridge:** The New Zealand freediver has a superstition related to words. He avoids saying certain words associated with danger or death before dives, believing they attract negative energy.

- **Tanya Streeter:** The British freediver always carries a small sea stone she found during her first deep dive. She considers this talisman a source of calm and focus during competitions.

- **Ahmed Gabr:** This Egyptian diver, who holds the record for the deepest dive with scuba gear, always performs a specific set of stretches in the same order before each deep dive to ward off bad luck.

- **Umberto Pelizzari:** The Italian freediver avoids eating certain foods, like fish or seafood, before an important dive. He believes eating sea creatures before diving brings bad luck and a lack of connection with the ocean.

- **François Sarano:** The French oceanographer always places a turtle figurine on his diving gear before a major dive, believing that this animal will safely guide him through exploration.

- **Zale Parry:** An American diving pioneer, Zale always carried a red handkerchief inside her diving suit. She believed this color offered additional protection during dives in unfamiliar waters.

- **Hans Hass:** The renowned diving pioneer and documentarian avoided diving on full moon days, as he believed this lunar phase altered currents and made dives more dangerous.

- **Jill Heinerth:** The cave diving expert follows a superstition of never turning her back to the entrance of a cave before starting a dive, considering it a sign of respect towards the environment she is about to explore.

- **Frederick Dumas:** One of the pioneers of scuba diving, he always wore an old diving watch during his explorations, even after it stopped working. He considered it his lucky charm and took it with him on all his major dives.

- **Franck Goddio:** This underwater archaeologist and diver, known for discovering significant archaeological remains like the sunken city of Heracleion in Egypt, has the superstition of always performing a small ritual of thanks to the ocean before any major dive. He believes this act is essential for successful explorations.

- **Pascal Bernabé:** This French technical diver, who holds a record for deep scuba diving, never dives without his personal weight belt, the same one he used during his first dives. He believes that changing gear for an important dive could bring bad luck.

- **Nuno Gomes:** The South African known for his deep diving records always carries an old coin in his wetsuit pocket. He found this coin during one of his first dives, and it has become his good luck charm.

- **Pipín Ferreras:** The famous Cuban freediver who reached great depths without breathing equipment had a superstition of never wearing brightly colored clothing before a dive. He believed that flashy colors attracted bad luck and broke his concentration.

43

Famous quotes.

1. Jacques Cousteau (France)

 - "The sea, once it casts its spell, holds one in its net of wonders forever."
 - "For most people, the sky is the limit. For those of us who love underwater exploration, the ocean is our home."
 - "We forget that the water cycle and the cycle of life are one."

2. Herbert Nitsch (Austria)

 - "Underwater, there is no sound or distraction, only the stillness of the depths."
 - "The body is more capable than we imagine. Diving is a matter of self-confidence."
 - "Breathe, relax, and anything is possible underwater."

3. Enzo Maiorca (Italy)

 - "The ocean is not just water; it is the mirror of life itself."
 - "Every dive is a conversation with the sea, where every bubble tells a story."
 - "Underwater, I feel more alive than on the surface."

4. Guillaume Néry (France)

 - "Diving is like flying. The ocean is the sky for those who dream in blue."
 - "Water teaches me to find balance and be patient."
 - "It's not about how deep you can go, but how you connect with the ocean."

5. William Trubridge (New Zealand)

 - "Diving is a dance with the abyss, a union with the depths."
 - "The key lies in the mind, in calmness. The body follows the soul."
 - "The sea is the last place where one can feel true freedom."

6. Umberto Pelizzari (Italy)

 - "Freediving is more than a sport, it's a way of life. Underwater, we are more human than on the surface."
 - "The sea has taught me to live in the present, to trust my breath, and to follow my heart."
 - "Every time I dive, I rediscover my connection with nature."

7. Natalia Molchanova (Russia)

 - "The sea has given me more than I could ever give back. It is my home, my refuge."
 - "In the water, I find the peace I always sought on the surface."
 - "To dive, you need more heart than lungs."

8. Pipín Ferreras (Cuba)

 - "The ocean is my soulmate, an eternal lover to whom I always return."
 - "Every dive is a dialogue with death, where life always has the final word."
 - "Fear exists to be conquered. Underwater, I am invincible."

9. Tanya Streeter (Cayman Islands)

- "The ocean is a place of power. Every dive is an opportunity to reconnect with what truly matters."
- "Underwater, I find a freedom that cannot be described, only felt."
- "The sea is not an enemy; it is an ally. You just have to learn to listen to it."

10. Alberto Novelli (Italy)

- "Diving is not just a skill; it is a way of understanding the world."
- "When I'm underwater, time stops. All that matters is the next breath."
- "The ocean has given me a life I never thought possible."

11. Francisco "Pipín" Rodríguez (Cuba)

- "Water is my air, my refuge, and my peace."
- "It's not the depth that matters, but how you return to the surface."
- "The sea teaches me to be humble and to respect the unknown."

12. Carlos Coste (Venezuela)

- "Underwater, we are who we are—no masks, just the truth of life and death."
- "Pressure exists not only in the ocean but also in life. Learning to handle it is key."
- "Diving has shown me that limits are mental, not physical."

13. Christian Redl (Austria)

- "The ocean has taught me to be patient, to understand that life has its own rhythm."

- "Every dive is a return to the origin, a reconnection with something primal."
- "Underwater, silence is the most powerful language."

14. Ashley Chapman (United States)

- "Diving is a conversation with the soul. It's not about the depth, but what you find along the way."
- "The ocean is my teacher; it has taught me more about myself than anything else."
- "Breathing underwater is a gift, a blessing that connects you to something greater."

15. Benoît Lecomte (France)

- "The ocean is infinite, but the greatest thing you will find there is yourself."
- "Every stroke, every dive, brings me closer to the truth of who we are."
- "Diving is a dialogue with nature, where respect is the most important thing."

16. Pierre Frolla (Monaco)

- "The sea is the only place where my mind and body synchronize in complete harmony."
- "Every time I dive, the ocean teaches me a new lesson in humility."
- "Breathing underwater is an art, an art that connects you to the depths of life."

17. Davide Carrera (Italy)

- "Underwater, there is no space for the ego, only for the truth of who you are."

- "Diving has taught me to listen, to feel the rhythm of the sea, and to follow it."
- "Every dive is an opportunity to leave behind the noise of the world and find inner peace."

18. Alexey Molchanov (Russia)

- "Freediving is like meditating in motion; it's a journey inward."
- "The ocean is not just water, it is life itself manifesting in its purest form."
- "Every time I dive, I feel like the ocean gives me back something I lost on the surface."

19. Frederic Buyle (Belgium)

- "Diving is my religion, my way of connecting with something higher."
- "Underwater, the world becomes simple; all that matters is the next breath."
- "The ocean has taught me to respect, to listen, and to learn something new every day."

20. Mehgan Heaney-Grier (United States)

- "Each dive is a journey into the unknown, but also into oneself."
- "Diving is like flying, but in a deep blue sky where only you decide how far to go."
- "The sea is my sanctuary; it's where I feel most alive and at peace."

44

Movies and series about diving.

- The Abyss (1989): Directed by James Cameron, this science fiction film focuses on a team of divers who discover an alien life form in the ocean's depths. With a blend of underwater exploration and dramatic tension, "The Abyss" is one of the most iconic films depicting deep-sea diving.

- Into the Blue (2005): Starring Paul Walker and Jessica Alba, this action film is set in the waters of the Bahamas, where a group of friends, while diving, stumble upon a sunken treasure and criminals who want to claim it. It combines diving, adventure, and spectacular underwater landscapes.

- The Deep (1977): Based on the novel by Peter Benchley, the film follows a couple who discover a cargo of morphine and treasure in the depths of the sea while diving in Bermuda. It showcases both the beauty and danger of deep-sea diving.

- Sanctum (2011): This adventure thriller produced by James Cameron follows a team of cave divers trapped in an underground system after a storm. As they struggle to find a way out, they are forced to make life-or-death decisions underwater.

- The Blue Planet (BBC, 2001): This BBC documentary is one of the most comprehensive productions on marine life and the wonders of the underwater world. With stunning footage of the world's oceans, "The Blue Planet" is a masterpiece that captures the diversity of marine life.

- OceanMen: Extreme Dive (2001): A documentary about the lives and experiences of two of the world's best freedivers: Pipin Ferreras and Umberto Pelizzari. The film explores freediving, showcasing the extremes of the sport and the physical and mental challenges it entails.

- Le Grand Bleu (The Big Blue) (1988): A cult film directed by Luc Besson that follows the story of two freedivers and their personal and professional rivalry. It blends stunning underwater scenery with an emotional narrative about the relationship between humans and the ocean.

- Mission Blue (2014): A documentary focusing on the life and work of Sylvia Earle, one of the world's most renowned marine biologists. The film follows her mission to save the world's oceans and her relentless efforts to raise awareness about marine conservation.

- Black Water: Abyss (2020): This thriller revolves around a group of friends exploring an underwater cave system in Australia, only to find themselves trapped by a crocodile in the depths. It highlights the terror that can arise from the most unexpected situations during diving.

- Open Water (2003): Inspired by true events, this film tells the story of a couple of divers who are accidentally left behind by their boat in the middle of the ocean. They must face isolation, fear, and sharks in a dive that turns into a nightmare.

45

**Diving in underwater sulfur springs is
a remarkable experience that can be found in
places like the Caribbean Sea, where these natural
emissions create a unique and exotic environment.**

These sulfur springs emit bubbles and gases such as hydrogen sulfide from fissures on the seafloor, creating an entirely different aquatic landscape, with bubbles rising from the bottom and tinting the water in varying colors, including yellows, greens, and sometimes darker shades.

This phenomenon is often found in volcanic or geothermal underwater areas.

The sulfur springs not only produce visible bubbles but also cause changes in water temperature, which can impact local marine fauna and flora.

Some marine species have adapted to these extreme environments, although marine life around these springs is usually limited due to the toxicity of the surroundings.

The waters around these springs can be lethal if not approached with caution, as hydrogen sulfide and other chemical compounds dissolved in the water are potentially toxic to humans.

Divers venturing into these areas need to be especially cautious about the water conditions, as prolonged exposure to toxic gases or highly acidic water can lead to serious health issues, such as chemical burns or respiratory difficulties.

Additionally, it is crucial for diving equipment to be in perfect condition to prevent toxic water from coming into contact with the skin or lungs.

Some divers have experienced equipment deterioration due to the acidity of the waters near these springs, emphasizing the importance of having specialized and well-maintained gear for this type of dive.

Despite the risks, diving in these areas remains an appealing experience for those seeking a unique adventure.

The geological formations and sulfur bubbles create an almost surreal landscape, described by some divers as "walking on another planet."

However, improper handling of this type of dive can be dangerous, requiring proper training and thorough planning to minimize risks and ensure safety.

46

Diving in Mayan cenotes, located in Mexico's Yucatán Peninsula, offers a unique experience both geologically and historically.

Cenotes are natural freshwater sinkholes formed by the erosion of limestone, creating cavities that, in some cases, connect to extensive underwater cave systems.

For the ancient Mayans, cenotes were considered sacred places, serving as both sources of water and ceremonial sites.

Diving in these cenotes not only allows one to admire their extraordinary natural beauty but also to discover a piece of Mayan history and culture.

One of the most impressive aspects of cenote diving is the clarity of the water, which is extremely crystalline due to the natural filtration through the limestone.

This provides spectacular visibility, enabling divers to explore intricate cave systems and observe stalactites and stalagmites that have developed over thousands of years.

These underwater structures, slowly formed by the accumulation of minerals, create almost mystical landscapes underwater, where sunlight penetrates through openings, creating a surreal visual effect.

In addition to the geological formations, some cenotes also contain historical artifacts.

The Mayans used these sinkholes for sacred rituals, and in some cases, remains of offerings have been found, including pottery, tools, and even human remains dating back to the pre-Hispanic era.

Archaeologists and divers have documented significant discoveries in cenotes like the Sacred Cenote at Chichén Itzá, where it is believed that the Mayans threw offerings and sacrifices to honor the gods.

Diving in cenotes comes with challenges, as many of them are part of complex cave systems that can be difficult to navigate, requiring advanced cave diving skills.

Divers must be well-trained and equipped to move safely in these often dark and narrow underground spaces.

Orientation and planning are essential to avoid getting lost, as some cave networks can extend for several kilometers underground.

Examples of popular cenotes for diving include the Gran Cenote, Dos Ojos, and Cenote Angelita, each with its unique features.

In Dos Ojos, divers can explore an extensive underwater cave with passages stretching over several kilometers, while in Cenote Angelita, divers can descend to a cloud of hydrogen sulfide at 30 meters deep, creating the illusion of flying over an underground river.

Many divers describe their dives in cenotes as almost mystical experiences, as the combination of Mayan history, impressive geological structures, and the feeling of immersion in an underground world completely isolated from the outside creates an unmatched atmosphere.

47

Diving in subduction zones is a unique experience due to the intense geological activity that occurs where tectonic plates collide and slide beneath one another.

In these areas, divers can observe a range of impressive phenomena, such as gas bubbles being released, hydrothermal vents, and, in some cases, small active underwater volcanoes.

These bubbles can contain carbon dioxide or methane, and while they are often harmless at first glance, they can alter the water's chemistry, making it more acidic or even toxic if not approached with caution.

Diving in these zones not only offers spectacular views of geothermal activity but also poses risks due to sudden changes in water temperature and the potential release of toxic gases.

In some areas, such as the Mediterranean Sea near Greece and the Pacific in regions like Japan and the coast of Chile, divers have reported seeing sulfur vents that create columns of bubbles and mineral deposits, giving the underwater landscape an almost extraterrestrial appearance.

A notable example of this type of diving occurs in the Bay of Fundy Marine National Park, Canada, where gas bubbles can be observed emanating from tectonic faults.

Another interesting case is found in the Tonga subduction zone in the Pacific Ocean.

There, some divers have documented phenomena such as eruptions of small underwater volcanoes and the formation of sediment mounds that slowly shift.

However, due to the instability of these zones and the risk of underwater volcanic eruptions, diving in subduction areas requires careful planning and often the company of experienced guides.

Hot currents or gas bubbles can also disorient divers, making constant vigilance essential, along with the use of appropriate equipment to protect against sudden changes in pressure and temperature.

48

Diving with walruses is an uncommon yet fascinating experience, primarily taking place in the Arctic regions where these massive marine mammals reside.

Walruses, known for their long tusks and imposing size, can be curious creatures, but they can also be dangerous if they feel threatened or cornered.

Weighing up to 1,500 kilograms, they are among the largest animals a diver can encounter underwater.

Diving in the presence of walruses requires thorough preparation and a high level of caution.

While these animals are generally peaceful and more interested in their surroundings than in humans, they can become aggressive if they feel their space is being invaded.

Walruses use their tusks not only for defense but also to maneuver on ice and get out of the water, which gives them significant strength that could be dangerous to a nearby diver.

Some divers have reported encounters with walruses in places such as the Canadian Arctic, Greenland, Norway, and Alaska, where walruses search for food-rich areas, especially clam beds, which are their main source of sustenance.

During dives, these creatures may approach out of curiosity, but they can also move quickly to escape or intimidate if they feel uncomfortable.

A real example occurred in the Barents Sea, north of Norway, where a team of scientific divers encountered a group of walruses.

While they were initially friendly, a dominant male began to exhibit aggressive behavior when the divers got too close to the calves, forcing the team to retreat quickly.

Another challenge of diving with walruses is the environment itself.

The Arctic regions present extreme conditions of cold, limited visibility, and floating ice, adding significant risk.

The diving equipment in these areas must be specially designed to withstand low temperatures, and divers must be prepared to surface quickly if needed.

Using high-quality dry suits is essential to protect against the cold, but divers must also be aware of movements under the ice, which can shift rapidly and complicate the return to the surface.

In terms of safety, local guides and experienced divers recommend keeping a safe distance from the walruses and never positioning yourself between them and the water, as this is their primary escape route.

Walruses are social animals often found in large groups, and approaching one of them may trigger a defensive response from the entire group.

Diving with walruses is undoubtedly one of the most thrilling experiences in Arctic environments, but it is also one of the most dangerous.

49

Diving in the "brine layer" is one of the most unusual and fascinating experiences in deep diving.

These bodies of water, known as brine pools, are found at the bottom of the oceans and are extremely dense zones due to their high concentration of salt and other minerals.

These underwater "pools" create an incredible visual effect, as if there were a separate lake within the ocean, with a clear surface that often appears impossible to penetrate.

The difference in density between ocean water and brine creates an almost physical barrier that is challenging to break through, even for experienced divers.

Brine pools are mainly found in areas such as the Gulf of Mexico and the Mediterranean Sea, in regions with high concentrations of salt deposits beneath the seafloor.

These salt deposits originate from ancient seas that evaporated, leaving behind large amounts of salt, which have been covered by sediments over time.

Seawater slowly filters through these sediments, dissolving the salt and forming these dense lakes on the seafloor.

Due to its high salinity, the brine is so dense that objects, or even divers, float on its surface as if they were in the Dead Sea.

These brine pools are not only interesting for their appearance and composition but also for the unique ecosystems they host.

The conditions in these bodies of water are extremely hostile for most forms of life, as the high salt concentration and lack of oxygen create a toxic environment.

Nevertheless, certain extremophiles, such as bacteria and archaea, have evolved to survive in these environments.

These microorganisms feed on chemical compounds in the brine water and, in some cases, form part of food chains that involve larger organisms found in the nearby seafloor.

The life around these brine pools is limited but fascinating for its ability to adapt to such an extreme environment.

From a diving perspective, one of the biggest challenges is the difference in buoyancy and the way divers interact with the brine's surface.

Divers attempting to penetrate these lakes often find that their equipment is affected by the water's density, as buoyancy is much higher than in normal seawater.

In some cases, divers may feel like they are "bouncing" off the surface of the brine, unable to submerge.

This can be disorienting and requires adjustments in diving techniques.

A famous example of brine pool exploration occurred in the Gulf of Mexico, where a team of researchers discovered what they called the "Jacuzzi of Despair."

This underwater brine lake was not only impenetrable but also highly toxic.

Any animal that ventured into its waters, such as fish or crabs, would not survive, remaining preserved at the bottom.

The scientists were able to film this strange and lethal underwater lake, observing how organisms actively avoided its waters.

Another peculiarity of these brine lakes is that they are often surrounded by methane columns and gas bubbles rising from the seabed.

This adds another level of mystery and beauty to the scene, as the bubbles can create a surreal visual effect.

However, these areas are also hazardous for divers, as methane can be toxic and potentially flammable.

Diving into the "brine layer" is not a common experience, and due to the extreme conditions and the depth at which these lakes are found, this type of dive is usually reserved for scientific divers and specialized teams.

The equipment needed for these dives includes dry suits and advanced breathing systems, as the conditions can be very cold and the water highly corrosive.

50

Hyperbaric medicine, used in diving and other areas of healthcare, is a technique in which patients are treated in a hyperbaric chamber, an environment where they are provided with pure oxygen at high pressure.

This technique has its roots in treating divers who suffer from decompression sickness, a condition that occurs when dissolved gases in the blood, like nitrogen, form bubbles due to a rapid decrease in pressure during a fast ascent.

In the hyperbaric chamber, high-pressure oxygen helps reduce these bubbles, allowing nitrogen to be safely reabsorbed and eliminated from the body.

Beyond its use in diving, hyperbaric medicine has proven effective in treating a variety of medical conditions.

Pure oxygen administered at high pressure significantly increases oxygen levels in the blood and tissues, promoting cell regeneration, stimulating the formation of new blood vessels, and fighting infections.

For this reason, hyperbaric treatments are used to heal difficult wounds, such as diabetic ulcers, severe burns, radiation injuries, and even to improve recovery times from complex surgeries.

In the case of chronic or infected wounds, which often have poor blood circulation and insufficient oxygen supply, the use of a hyperbaric chamber can revitalize damaged tissue.

The additional oxygen not only stimulates the growth of new tissue but also enhances the body's ability to fight bacterial infections, many of which thrive in low-oxygen environments.

Professional athletes have also turned to hyperbaric medicine as a recovery method, due to its ability to accelerate muscle repair and reduce inflammation after intense training or injuries.

In fact, its use has been documented in high-performance sports like soccer and cycling.

Over time, hyperbaric chambers have proven to be a versatile tool in treating a wide range of medical conditions beyond diving.

Although they are primarily known in the diving field, their application in other areas is rapidly growing, standing out as a key technique in regenerative medicine and in treating conditions that require an increased oxygen supply at the cellular level.

51

The "runny nose syndrome" is a fairly common condition among divers and occurs after a dive due to the combination of sinus pressure and prolonged exposure to water.

This pressure, along with temperature variations and the entry of small amounts of water into the nose, can irritate the mucous membranes, causing the sinuses to overreact and produce excess mucus.

The phenomenon is more frequent in those who dive regularly, as the constant pressure changes during immersion affect the paranasal sinuses and upper airways.

The duration of the runny nose can range from a few hours to, in some cases, an entire day, depending on individual sensitivity and diving conditions, such as water temperature and depth reached.

The runny nose is generally more common when a diver has performed several consecutive dives or has not fully adapted to the underwater pressure changes.

Although not dangerous, the runny nose can be bothersome and may sometimes be accompanied by mild nasal congestion or a feeling of pressure in the head.

Some divers who frequently experience this syndrome have adopted preventive measures, such as using nasal decongestant sprays before diving or nasal irrigation with saline solutions after diving to relieve symptoms.

In extreme cases, divers with pre-existing sinus problems, such as chronic sinusitis or infections, may find that the runny nose syndrome worsens, potentially requiring medical treatment to prevent complications.

In some cases, a runny nose may indicate that the sinus passages are not properly equalizing pressure during the dive, which could increase the risk of nasal or ear barotrauma.

It has been reported that some divers experience this issue more intensely when diving in cold waters, as the cold can constrict blood vessels in the nasal passages and worsen irritation.

However, with proper management and the use of correct equalization techniques, runny nose syndrome is a manageable problem for most divers.

52

The phenomenon known as the "pressure shadow" is a sensation that some divers experience when descending to significant depths.

This sensation occurs due to the physiological effects of water pressure on the human body as it goes deeper.

At greater depths, the pressure increases significantly, creating a feeling of weight or compression in different parts of the body, which some describe as a "shadow" or a force that envelops them.

Pressure at depth particularly affects the air-filled spaces of the body, such as the lungs, sinuses, and middle ear.

While these effects are expected and managed through equalization techniques (such as the Valsalva maneuver to balance ear pressure), the sensation of the "pressure shadow" can be a more subjective and psychological experience.

For some divers, it manifests as a feeling that something invisible is "pushing" or "surrounding" them, while the aquatic environment feels denser and more oppressive.

Physically, the pressure can also cause the wetsuit to fit more tightly against the body, contributing to this perception of being "compressed" or "trapped."

Some divers report that the sensation of the "pressure shadow" intensifies in colder waters or during longer dives, where the body must constantly adapt to changes in pressure and temperature.

However, this feeling is part of the experience of deep diving, and for most experienced divers, it is accepted as part of the challenge and excitement of exploring the depths.

In some cases, this sensation can even contribute to a greater connection with the underwater environment, as divers develop a heightened physical awareness of the surroundings and changing conditions as they descend beyond 30 meters.

The "pressure shadow" itself is not dangerous, but it can cause a sense of anxiety or discomfort in some divers, especially if they are not accustomed to deep dives.

In such cases, dive instructors often recommend calm breathing techniques and gradual acclimatization to the pressure to avoid sensory overload.

53

The mirror effect underwater is an optical phenomenon that occurs when the water's surface reflects images of the seabed or the diver like a mirror.

This effect happens under specific light and angle conditions, usually when the water is clear and calm, and the diver is looking up toward the surface from an almost perpendicular position.

Light hitting the water's surface reflects rather than passing through, creating an inverted image of what is below.

This phenomenon can be disorienting because, from the diver's perspective, it seems as if two worlds overlap: the real one beneath the water and a reflected one that appears to float above them.

This reflection can show both the seabed and other divers, or even the diver themselves, creating a feeling of seeing a double, which can cause temporary confusion regarding spatial orientation.

While the mirror effect is more common in calm, shallow waters, it can also be observed in deeper waters if conditions are favorable, such as in underwater caves or clear lakes.

For some divers, this phenomenon adds a fascinating element to the experience, creating an almost magical or surreal atmosphere.

However, for others, it can be unsettling, especially if they are already disoriented due to the lack of clear visual reference points in the underwater environment.

54

Pearl diving is an ancient tradition dating back thousands of years, practiced in various parts of the world, particularly in the Persian Gulf, Japan, and some Southeast Asian countries.

Initially, pearl seekers performed dives using apnea, meaning without breathing equipment.

These divers would plunge to great depths to collect oysters that contained the valuable pearls inside.

In the Persian Gulf, the pearl diving industry was one of the main sources of income until the early 20th century.

Pearl divers in this region, known as "haamli", would descend to depths between 10 and 30 meters, relying solely on a rope tied to a boat.

They did not use protective or breathing equipment, depending only on their lung capacity and physical endurance.

To protect themselves from saltwater and possible jellyfish stings, they would cover their nostrils with clips and use wax to cover their ears.

An experienced diver could perform up to 50 dives in a single day, gathering as many oysters as possible before returning to the surface.

This work was extremely dangerous.

Divers constantly faced the threat of shark attacks, the risk of fainting due to lack of oxygen, and the danger of decompression from ascending too quickly.

Despite these dangers, the allure of finding a valuable pearl drove many to continue this practice.

In Japan, the tradition of the *ama*, female pearl divers, is equally legendary, as these women have been diving without breathing equipment since ancient times to collect pearls, shellfish, and seaweed.

Although technology has advanced, some "ama" still practice this tradition today, preserving a craft deeply connected to local culture.

Over time, the introduction of more modern and safer methods, such as the use of oxygen tanks and the cultivation of oysters on specialized farms, has changed the landscape of pearl collection.

Modern pearl production mainly focuses on cultured pearls, especially since Mikimoto Kokichi, a Japanese entrepreneur, perfected the technique of cultivating pearls in the late 19th century.

Today, cultured pearls make up the majority of the market, and wild pearl diving has significantly declined.

However, in some places like the Persian Gulf, traditions still endure.

Local divers continue to perform dives as a way to connect with their cultural roots, and there are even annual festivals that celebrate this ancient practice.

55

Diving in "dead zones" is a haunting and desolate experience, as these ocean areas are extremely low in oxygen, making marine life scarce or nonexistent.

"Dead zones" are areas of the ocean where dissolved oxygen levels are so low that marine organisms cannot survive, resulting in an empty and barren ecosystem.

These hypoxic zones have been identified in several parts of the world, but one of the largest and most well-known is in the Gulf of Mexico, where marine life either dies or flees due to the lack of oxygen.

Dead zones are primarily caused by eutrophication, a process in which excess nutrients, typically from agricultural runoff and industrial waste, enter the ocean and trigger explosive algal growth.

When these algae die, they sink and are decomposed by bacteria that consume large amounts of oxygen in the process.

This creates areas where oxygen levels are so low that fish, crustaceans, and other organisms cannot survive, leaving vast stretches of the seabed barren.

For divers exploring these areas, the experience can be unsettling.

The absence of visible life, often murky waters, and the lack of natural ecosystem activity generate a strange and almost surreal atmosphere.

Instead of the vibrant coral reefs or schools of fish typically found in healthy ocean areas, divers in dead zones may encounter a lifeless marine landscape, sometimes with the seafloor covered in layers of mud and decomposing organic matter.

A notable example of a dead zone is the one that forms annually in the Gulf of Mexico.

During the summer months, a vast expanse of waters off the coast of Louisiana and Texas becomes a dead zone, sometimes reaching up to 20,000 square kilometers.

This dead zone is a direct result of agricultural pollution, primarily fertilizers that flow into rivers and eventually drain into the Gulf.

The size and severity of the zone vary from year to year, but it remains one of the largest and most well-studied in the world.

In some cases, scientific divers explore these areas to study the effects of environmental changes on ocean ecosystems.

Despite the harsh conditions, diving in dead zones can provide valuable data on the impact of pollution and the long-term effects of declining oxygen levels in the ocean.

There have also been reports of sightings of certain marine species that adapt to these extreme conditions, offering important insights into the resilience of marine life.

Divers who have experienced it describe a sense of emptiness and desolation, with dark, murky waters, no visible life, and a monotonous underwater landscape.

56

The "twilight zone," also known as the mesopelagic zone, is an oceanic region that extends from 200 to 1,000 meters in depth.

In this zone, sunlight barely penetrates, creating a constant dimness that gives it its name.

At these depths, the ocean becomes an extremely inhospitable environment, with low temperatures and significantly higher pressure than at the surface.

Due to these extreme conditions, exploration of the twilight zone has been limited, and only the most experienced technical divers and unmanned underwater vehicles, such as autonomous submarines, can access it.

Diving in the twilight zone not only requires advanced diving skills but also specific equipment that can withstand the intense pressures and ensure the diver's survival.

Special gas mixtures, such as trimix or heliox, are essential to prevent issues like nitrogen narcosis or oxygen toxicity at these depths.

Moreover, dives in this region require careful decompression planning, as a rapid ascent can lead to decompression sickness or barotrauma.

The fauna of the twilight zone is unique and often bioluminescent, meaning that they emit their own light through chemical reactions.

Some examples include lanternfish and glow-in-the-dark squid, creating an astonishing visual display in the ocean's depths.

These organisms have developed extraordinary adaptations to survive in near-total darkness, using bioluminescence not only to communicate or attract prey but also to camouflage themselves from predators.

The ecosystem in the twilight zone is completely different from that of surface waters.

Animals living here tend to be large predators, such as giant squid, dragonfish, and other species capable of feeding on smaller creatures that vertically migrate at night from the depths toward the surface in search of food.

These daily vertical movements, known as the largest mass migration on the planet, are crucial for the oceanic carbon cycle, as they transfer nutrients between the ocean's surface and deep layers.

Real examples of exploration in the twilight zone include scientific expeditions conducted by the Alvin submersible or the ROV Deep Discoverer, which have descended to these depths to film and study the ecosystem.

In 2020, the manned research submarine DSV Limiting Factor, used in the Five Deeps Expedition, explored the mesopelagic zone in various parts of the world.

This mission revealed fascinating details about species living in extreme conditions and helped uncover some of the mysteries of this underexplored region.

Studies conducted in the twilight zone have revealed that this region of the ocean plays a crucial role in regulating the planet's climate, as it acts as a significant carbon sink.

The creatures living here capture carbon through feeding and waste, and this carbon sinks deeper into the ocean, reducing the amount of carbon dioxide in the atmosphere.

Despite technological advancements and the use of unmanned vehicles allowing more detailed exploration of the twilight zone, much remains to be discovered.

Technological limitations and the high costs of expeditions mean that much of this zone remains a mystery.

However, each new dive reveals more about the biodiversity, geology, and biological processes occurring at these depths.

57

In some tropical areas, "cleaner fish" play a fundamental role in underwater ecosystems by cleaning other fish of parasites and dead skin.

These small fish, such as cleaner wrasses and some gobies, establish "cleaning stations" where larger fish stop to be cleaned.

Surprisingly, these cleaner fish can also approach divers, as if mistaking them for other fish, and attempt to clean their diving gear or even exposed skin.

This fascinating behavior has been observed by divers in places like the Red Sea, the Maldives, and other tropical regions with abundant marine life.

The cleaner fish swim around the diver, inspecting the diving equipment in search of something to eat, as they would with a larger fish.

While harmless, it can be a curious and amusing experience for divers, as they feel the gentle touches of these small fish as they diligently "clean."

This behavior highlights the importance of symbiotic relationships in marine ecosystems and how these natural interactions can extend to humans who dive into this world.

Cleaner fish provide a crucial service by maintaining the health of other fish, removing parasites and debris that could cause infections or diseases.

Moreover, the opportunity to witness this type of interaction up close is one of the many attractions that make diving in tropical areas a unique experience.

Some divers have reported that these cleaner fish not only limit themselves to cleaning the equipment but even gently nibble on exposed areas of the skin, such as hands or ankles, in an attempt to perform their natural job.

While not a dangerous interaction, it can be surprising and even ticklish for divers who don't expect this attention from the small marine cleaners.

This connection between cleaner fish and divers is a reminder of how nature interacts with all beings around it, adapting and responding to new situations, even in the underwater world.

58

People can experience cramps during diving for various reasons, with muscle fatigue, dehydration, lack of warm-up, and cold being the main causes.

While submerged, the body loses heat more quickly, which can create tension in the muscles and lead to cramps, especially in the legs or feet.

Dehydration is another common cause, as cold water and breathing through the regulator can make divers lose fluids without realizing it, affecting the balance of electrolytes like sodium and potassium, which are essential for proper muscle function.

Muscle fatigue is also a significant factor since divers use muscles in ways that may be unfamiliar, such as fin movements, leading to overexertion and eventually cramps.

Additionally, if a diver hasn't warmed up properly before diving, the lack of adequate blood flow in the muscles increases the risk of cramping.

To prevent cramps while diving, it's essential to stay hydrated before and during the activity, as well as perform stretches and warm-ups to prepare the muscles.

It's also advisable to maintain good finning technique and avoid unnecessary overexertion.

If a cramp occurs during the dive, it's recommended to stretch the affected muscle slowly, try to relax, and not panic to continue the dive safely.

59

Common hand signals in diving.

- **Ok (I'm fine):** Form a circle with the thumb and index finger while the other three fingers are extended.

- **Problem / Not okay:** Flatten the hand and move it side to side (as if "waving" the hand).

- **Ascend:** Thumbs up with a closed fist.

- **Descend:** Thumbs down with a closed fist.

- **Stop:** Open, flat hand with the palm facing forward, signaling "stop."

- **Low on air:** Tap the chest with a closed fist.

- **Share air:** Point to the emergency regulator (octopus) with the hand.

- **Adjust buoyancy:** Move palms up or down slowly.

- **Need help:** Wave an extended arm above the head.

- **Look at me / attention:** Point to your own eyes with the index finger.

- **Swim in that direction:** Extend the arm and point with the index finger in the desired direction.

- **"I need air":** Place the hand on the throat as if cutting off air, indicating low air supply.

- **Something's wrong:** Make a claw shape with the hand and move it near the mouth or equipment (often indicating equipment issues).

- **Ear problem:** Touch the ears repeatedly.

- **Strong wind / rough conditions:** Hit the edge of the hand repeatedly against the open palm.

- **Boat nearby:** Move an open hand with fingers extended up and down, simulating a boat on water.

- **Danger:** Make a fist with the hand and extend the arm outward.

- **Gather the group:** Move the hand in a circular motion to gather the divers.

- **Good visibility:** Give a "thumbs up" gesture with an extended hand, moving it gently.

- **Poor visibility:** Make a large circle in the air with the hand, then point downward.

- **Time to exit:** Tap the wrist or hand as if checking a watch.

- **Low air reserve:** Make a "T" with both hands.

- **Shark warning:** Extend the hand with the thumb on the forehead (like a fin).

- **Jellyfish warning:** Extend fingers and move hands to simulate jellyfish tentacles.

- **Seahorse:** Curve the index finger and thumb.

- Octopus: Move both hands with fingers extended, simulating the tentacles of an octopus.

 - Big fish: Place both open hands on either side of the head, as if describing the size of a fish.

 - Lobster: Wiggle the fingers up and down to mimic lobster claws.

 - Turtle: Place one hand on top of the other with thumbs extended and moving, imitating a turtle.

 - Manta ray: Extend open arms to the sides and move them like the fins of a manta ray.

 - Snake or eel: Move the index finger in a zigzag motion, mimicking the movement of a snake.

 - "Go there": Point with the finger in the direction you want to go.

 - "Low air": Show the number 2 with your fingers (index and middle) and move them back and forth, indicating that the air reserve is decreasing.

60

The white light we perceive at the surface is composed of different colors corresponding to the visible spectrum: red, orange, yellow, green, blue, indigo, and violet.

When diving, the behavior of light changes dramatically due to the water's ability to absorb and scatter the different wavelengths of light as depth increases.

This phenomenon causes colors to disappear progressively as one descends.

The first colors to be absorbed are those with longer wavelengths, starting with red at about 5 meters deep.

Red completely disappears, and any object of this color begins to appear grayish or black.

Next, orange and yellow fade, generally around 10 to 20 meters.

At greater depths, green tones start to dominate, and the scenery becomes more monochromatic and bluish, as blue is the color that penetrates the water the farthest.

This process continues until, at depths of 50 or 60 meters, the environment becomes almost entirely monochromatic with a predominant dark blue hue.

Beyond this point, darkness increases significantly, and color perception is nearly nonexistent without the help of an artificial light source.

For divers, carrying a flashlight is essential, especially during deep dives or in underwater caves, as artificial light allows the original colors absorbed by the water to "return."

When objects are illuminated underwater, their original colors suddenly reappear, restoring the vibrant tones that the water had removed.

For example, a red fish that appeared gray without light will show its characteristic color again when lit with a flashlight.

This phenomenon is also relevant for underwater photography.

When taking photos at great depths without an additional light source, images tend to have a bluish or greenish hue.

Professional underwater photographers use powerful flashlights or external flashes to restore colors in their photos.

Additionally, they can use specific camera filters to correct the bluish tint, enhancing the capture of natural colors in deep waters.

In post-production, color correction is a common practice in editing underwater photos to make the colors look more realistic, vibrant, and balanced, compensating for the chromatic distortions caused by water depth.

61

To prevent your dive mask from fogging up more effectively, there are several lasting methods you can apply, beyond spitting on the lenses or using biodegradable detergents.

1. New Mask Pre-Treatment:

When you get a new mask, the lenses often have a thin layer of silicone or manufacturing residue that promotes fogging.

To remove this layer:

 - Use toothpaste (not gel): Apply a small amount of toothpaste to the inside of the lenses and gently rub it with your fingers. Let the toothpaste sit on the lenses for a few minutes before rinsing thoroughly with warm water. This method will help remove silicone residue and improve visibility. Avoid using abrasive products that could scratch the lenses.

2. Heat Treatment: Another common method is to lightly burn the inner surface of the lenses with a lighter to remove any silicone residue. Carefully run a lighter's flame over the inner surface of the lenses until a slight fog forms. Be sure not to burn the silicone around the lenses or apply too much heat. Then, let it cool and rinse thoroughly with warm water to remove the burned residue.

3. Commercial Anti-Fog Solutions:

There are specific products on the market, such as anti-fog sprays or gels, that create a protective layer on the lenses.

These products are formulated to keep the mask fog-free during dives.

4. Keep the mask rinsed in warm water before diving: Before each dive, rinse your mask in warm or room-temperature water. This will help equalize the temperature of the glass with the water, preventing condensation that causes fogging.

5. Avoid breathing through your nose while diving: A common cause of fogging is inadvertently breathing through the nose, which creates more moisture inside the mask. Maintain control over your breathing to avoid this issue.

6. Continuous defogging during the dive: If you're already submerged and your mask starts to fog up, a common method is to let a small amount of water into the mask, move it around slightly, and use the water to clear the lenses. Then, expel the water by blowing through your nose, keeping the visor fog-free.

62

Sea snakes are a fascinating group of reptiles that inhabit the oceans, primarily in the Indian Ocean and the Western Pacific, especially around the northern coasts of Australia, Southeast Asia, and the Indo-Pacific islands.

There are over fifty species of sea snakes, and all of them are venomous, although they are not aggressive toward humans, which minimizes the risk of dangerous encounters.

These reptiles are perfectly adapted to marine life.

Unlike their terrestrial relatives, sea snakes have a flattened tail that allows them to swim efficiently, using it as a rudder.

However, like other reptiles, they must breathe air, so they need to surface regularly.

This means that although they can remain submerged for long periods, ranging from 30 minutes to over an hour, they must ascend to breathe before returning to the depths.

The venom of sea snakes is very potent and is primarily designed to immobilize their prey, which usually consists of small fish, crustaceans, and mollusks.

However, despite being venomous, they rarely attack humans.

Divers who have encountered sea snakes often describe them as curious but not aggressive.

Generally, if they feel threatened, they will try to flee rather than attack.

An important fact for divers is that sea snakes are more active in warm, shallow waters, where they search for food.

While encounters with them are not common, divers should remember that, as with any marine life, it is essential not to disturb or try to handle them.

Most bites occur when humans try to handle or catch the snakes, triggering a defensive reaction.

In terms of prevention, it is crucial for divers to maintain a respectful distance, avoid sudden movements that might startle them, and, above all, remember that these animals prefer to avoid conflict.

Diving in areas known to be inhabited by sea snakes requires caution, but the likelihood of an attack is very low if a respectful approach toward marine life is followed.

63

Water is an excellent thermal conductor, meaning it transfers heat from our bodies much more quickly than air.

Specifically, the rate of cold propagation in water is approximately 25 times faster than in air.

This happens because water has a higher density and thermal capacity, allowing it to absorb body heat more efficiently.

At an ambient temperature of 20°C in the air, we wouldn't feel cold, as our body can remain relatively insulated from the surroundings, but in water at the same temperature, we begin to feel cold almost immediately.

This is because body heat is lost rapidly through contact with water.

As we spend more time in the water, even at cool or moderate temperatures, we may start to feel an increasing sensation of cold and, eventually, hypothermia if protective gear like a wetsuit is not used.

The time it takes to feel cold depends on several factors, such as water temperature, exposure time, the thickness of the wetsuit (or if one is used at all), and the person's physical condition.

In 20°C water, a person may start to feel discomfort after a prolonged period, while at lower temperatures, the effects of cold are felt almost immediately.

64

Buoyancy in water is directly related to body density and the amount of body fat.

In general, women tend to float better than men because, biologically, they typically have a higher proportion of body fat compared to men.

Body fat has a lower density than water, which means it is lighter and tends to float.

As a result, women, having more body fat, have a greater capacity for buoyancy.

On the other hand, men generally have a higher percentage of muscle mass, which is denser than water and, therefore, does not contribute as much to buoyancy.

The muscular and bone density of the male body causes men to tend to sink faster in water if they do not make efforts to stay afloat.

The fact that women float better does not necessarily mean they are better swimmers, as efficiency in the water also depends on technique, strength, and endurance, but it does provide a natural advantage in terms of passive buoyancy.

This can also be beneficial in activities like diving or endurance swimming, where maintaining good buoyancy can help conserve energy.

This phenomenon is also linked to the distribution of fat in the body.

In women, fat tends to accumulate in the hips, thighs, and buttocks, which can help stabilize the body when in the water.

Additionally, factors such as age, the specific body composition of each person, and the type of training can influence this buoyancy capacity in both men and women.

65

It is not advisable to fly after a day of diving due to the risk of decompression sickness (also known as "the bends").

This occurs because, during a dive, nitrogen dissolves in the body's tissues as we breathe compressed air at greater depths.

At greater depths, the body absorbs more nitrogen due to increased pressure.

When ascending slowly, this dissolved nitrogen has time to be safely released through breathing.

However, if one ascends rapidly or flies shortly after diving, the pressure change can be too abrupt for the nitrogen to be safely released, forming bubbles inside the body.

These nitrogen bubbles can cause serious problems by disrupting blood flow and affecting the body's tissues and organs.

Symptoms of decompression sickness can include joint and muscle pain, fatigue, dizziness, mental confusion, breathing difficulties, and, in severe cases, paralysis or even death.

The risk increases during flights because, at high altitudes, atmospheric pressure decreases.

This drop in pressure can intensify the formation of nitrogen bubbles in the blood, worsening decompression symptoms.

To minimize these risks, experts recommend waiting a period of time before flying after a dive.

This waiting period depends on several factors, such as the depth of the dive, the number of dives performed, and whether they were decompression or non-decompression dives.

Standard guidelines suggest a minimum waiting time of 12 to 18 hours before boarding a flight, and in some cases, it may be necessary to wait up to 24 hours if deep or multiple dives were conducted.

The reason for this wait is to allow the remaining nitrogen in the body to be safely and gradually eliminated through breathing, preventing dangerous bubble formation as pressure decreases during the flight.

Ultimately, flying after diving without respecting this waiting time puts the diver at unnecessary risk of a condition that could have been easily avoided.

66

As you approach 30 meters of depth, the ambient pressure increases significantly, causing the body to absorb more dissolved nitrogen into the blood and tissues.

This phenomenon can lead to what is known as nitrogen narcosis, a temporary condition that affects the central nervous system and causes symptoms similar to intoxication or drunkenness.

Nitrogen narcosis, often called "the rapture of the deep," typically begins to manifest at around 30 meters of depth, although its onset and severity vary depending on the person and the dive.

As depth increases, the partial pressure of nitrogen also rises, causing the gas to have anesthetic effects on the brain.

Symptoms can include a feeling of euphoria, excessive relaxation, lack of concentration, impaired judgment, confusion, dizziness, and even hallucinations.

In more severe cases, divers may experience a sense of invulnerability or indifference to danger, which can lead to reckless or dangerous decisions underwater.

A key feature of nitrogen narcosis is that the symptoms quickly disappear when the diver ascends to a shallower depth.

By reducing the ambient pressure, the body releases the excess dissolved nitrogen, alleviating the effects of narcosis.

In this regard, the simplest solution is to ascend slightly, just a few meters, which generally alleviates the symptoms without causing long-term side effects.

However, if the diver continues descending beyond 30 meters without addressing the situation, the effects of narcosis can intensify.

At greater depths, the symptoms can become more severe, potentially leading to a total loss of control, disorientation, mental paralysis, or even unconsciousness.

In such cases, the situation can become extremely dangerous, as the diver may be unable to manage their equipment properly, forget safety rules, or lose spatial orientation, increasing the risk of serious or fatal accidents.

It is important to note that nitrogen narcosis not only depends on depth but also on other factors such as the diver's physical and psychological condition, level of experience, water temperature, and physical exertion during the dive.

Additionally, not all divers experience the same symptoms or the same intensity; some may not feel narcosis until greater depths, while others may notice it at 25 or 30 meters.

For divers who need to work at great depths for extended periods, such as in technical or commercial diving, a gas mix known as trimix or heliox can be used, which replaces some of the nitrogen with helium.

Helium has a less narcotic effect on the body, allowing for deeper dives without the dangers associated with nitrogen narcosis, though it is important to note that diving with these mixes requires specialized training.

67

The deepest place in the ocean is found in the Mariana Trench, an underwater abyss located in the Western Pacific near the Mariana Islands.

The deepest known point of this trench is the Challenger Deep, reaching an astonishing depth of approximately 10,994 meters (almost 11 kilometers).

This is the deepest place on Earth, exceeding the height of Mount Everest, which measures 8,848 meters above sea level, by more than 2,000 meters.

The bottom of the Challenger Deep is covered in total darkness and subjected to extremely high pressure, roughly 1,000 times greater than the pressure at sea level.

At these depths, conditions are incredibly hostile: no sunlight reaches this far, temperatures are near freezing, and the pressure is so high it would crush most organisms or any equipment not designed to withstand these extreme forces.

Despite the inhospitable environment, life has been discovered at these depths.

Creatures such as fish, shrimp, and unicellular organisms that have evolved to survive under these extreme conditions have been observed in the Mariana Trench.

Many of these organisms are unique and adapted to the lack of light, low temperatures, and high pressure.

To reach the bottom of the trench, a heavy object dropped from the surface would take about an hour to touch the seafloor.

However, the process of human and robotic exploration of these depths has been much more complex and slow.

Only a few specialized vehicles and submarines have reached the bottom of the Mariana Trench.

The first manned voyage to the Challenger Deep was made in 1960 by the bathyscaphe Trieste, carrying Swiss oceanographer Jacques Piccard and U.S. Navy Lieutenant Don Walsh.

Since then, only a few additional dives have taken place, one of the most recent being in 2012 by filmmaker James Cameron, who descended in a specially designed submarine.

At these extreme depths, the challenge of exploration lies not only in the crushing pressure but also in the total darkness and the inaccessible environment.

Advanced technologies, such as unmanned submarines and robotic systems, are essential for continuing to explore this environment.

As technology evolves, it is expected that we will be able to uncover more of the secrets held by this deep abyss, where many mysteries still remain unresolved.

Additionally, the Mariana Trench is one of the most fascinating places on the planet from a geological perspective.

It is located in a subduction zone, where the Pacific tectonic plate sinks beneath the Philippine plate, creating not only extreme depths but also geothermal phenomena such as underwater volcanoes and hydrothermal vents.

68

The popular perception of sharks as extremely dangerous creatures has been largely influenced by movies, media, and popular culture.

Movies like "Jaws" (1975) have instilled a widespread fear of these animals, even though the actual chances of being attacked by a shark are incredibly low.

In fact, in the United States, a person is more likely to be struck by lightning than bitten by a shark.

Statistics support this: shark attacks are extremely rare events, and most of them are not fatal.

Most of the time, sharks attack by mistake, confusing humans with potential prey.

In reality, sharks are fascinating creatures highly adapted to their environment.

One of their most remarkable features is their ability to detect minimal electric fields.

They achieve this through sensory organs called Ampullae of Lorenzini, located on their snouts, which allow them to pick up the electrical signals emitted by other living beings.

Even a flashlight turned on underwater can emit an electric field strong enough to be detected by a shark from several kilometers away.

This sense, known as electroreception, is a key tool for hunting, allowing sharks to locate prey in murky or dark waters where vision is not useful.

The Ampullae of Lorenzini are small pores filled with a gel-like substance that act as detectors of changes in electric fields.

This ability not only helps sharks hunt but also allows them to navigate the vast oceans using Earth's magnetic field.

Despite their image as fearsome predators, the reality is that many shark species are under severe threat due to overfishing and indiscriminate hunting for their fins, a common practice in the "shark finning" industry.

Sharks play an essential role in the marine ecosystem, maintaining the balance of food chains, making their conservation crucial for ocean health.

Additionally, sharks are highly diverse creatures, with over 500 known species, ranging from the gigantic whale shark, the largest fish in the world and a peaceful plankton filter-feeder, to smaller species like the dwarf lantern shark, which measures just 20 centimeters.

While some species, like the great white shark, have a more fearsome reputation, many others are harmless to humans.

Fear of sharks has led to a lack of understanding about their true nature and little emphasis on their conservation.

69

The amount of time a diver can stay underwater depends not only on the amount of oxygen available in the tank but also on the absorption of nitrogen that occurs as they descend to greater depths.

As a diver goes deeper, the ambient pressure increases, and this increase affects how the human body absorbs gases, such as nitrogen, which is present in the compressed air of diving tanks.

When a diver breathes compressed air at higher pressure (due to depth), nitrogen dissolves in body tissues in greater quantities than normal.

This process intensifies with increasing depth, as the partial pressure of gases is higher at greater depths.

Nitrogen itself is not toxic in small amounts, but as the body absorbs it, its accumulation can cause several problems if not managed properly.

The main risk associated with nitrogen absorption is decompression sickness, also known as "the bends" or decompression illness.

This condition occurs when a diver ascends too quickly after spending an extended time at a certain depth.

If the ascent is abrupt, the nitrogen dissolved in the tissues and blood does not have enough time to be gradually released through the lungs.

This can form bubbles in the body.

These bubbles can damage tissues and obstruct blood flow, leading to symptoms ranging from mild joint pain to paralysis or even death in severe cases.

For this reason, bottom time (i.e., how long a diver can stay at a certain depth) is limited not only by the oxygen carried in the tank but also by the amount of nitrogen the body can absorb without exceeding safety limits.

Decompression tables and dive computers are crucial tools for calculating safe dive times, as they indicate the depth and duration for safe diving without exceeding nitrogen saturation limits.

At greater depths, the amount of time a diver can stay at the bottom is significantly reduced.

For example, at a depth of 30 meters, the no-decompression time is considerably shorter than at a depth of 18 meters.

If a diver exceeds these times, they will need to perform decompression stops during the ascent to gradually release the dissolved nitrogen.

Additionally, if a diver uses gas mixtures other than air, such as nitrox (a mixture with more oxygen and less nitrogen), they can extend their bottom time, as the body will absorb less nitrogen.

However, this does not completely eliminate the risk of nitrogen absorption or decompression sickness.

70

The diving techniques employed by the navies of different countries are advanced and specialized due to the critical and often dangerous nature of their missions.

These techniques are designed to operate in extreme conditions, conduct combat missions, deactivate underwater explosives, perform underwater reconnaissance, rescue personnel, and carry out other high-risk tasks.

Main diving techniques used by the navy:

 - **Open-circuit diving:** This is the most common type of diving and is similar to recreational diving. Divers use self-contained underwater breathing apparatus (SCUBA), which expels exhaled air into the water. The main difference between recreational and military divers is the nature of the operations. Navy divers undertake longer and deeper dives and must be prepared to work in hostile conditions.

 - **Closed-circuit diving (rebreathers):** This technique is crucial for covert operations, as it allows divers to avoid producing visible bubbles, reducing the risk of detection. Rebreathers recycle exhaled air, remove carbon dioxide, and add oxygen as needed. These devices enable divers to breathe from the same air supply for longer periods and with greater stealth.

 - **Saturation diving:** Saturation diving is a technique used for prolonged missions at great depths, where divers may spend days or even weeks working underwater.

Instead of repeatedly ascending and descending, divers stay in pressurized chambers, where their bodies become saturated with dissolved gases like nitrogen. Once the mission is completed, the divers perform a single decompression, which can take several hours or even days. This type of diving is used for rescue, recovery, and repair operations at great depths.

- **Mixed-gas diving:** At greater depths, the normal breathing mixture (air) becomes dangerous due to oxygen toxicity and the narcotic effects of nitrogen. To address this, navy divers use gas mixtures like heliox (helium and oxygen) or trimix (helium, oxygen, and nitrogen), which allow for safe operations at extreme depths. These mixtures reduce the risks of nitrogen narcosis and oxygen toxicity, both of which can be fatal.

- **Surface-supplied breathing apparatus (SSBA):** In this technique, divers receive air or other gases from the surface through a long hose connected to a diving helmet or full-face mask. This technique allows divers to stay underwater longer than with SCUBA, as they are not dependent on air tanks. Additionally, divers can communicate with the surface through communication systems integrated into their helmets. This type of diving is commonly used for underwater construction, ship repair, and military structures.

- **Diving in contaminated water:** Military divers must be trained to dive in waters contaminated by chemicals, radiation, or biological hazards. For such operations, specially designed diving suits and breathing equipment are used to prevent contact with hazardous substances. These missions are extremely dangerous and require rigorous planning and training.

- Combat diving: Navy divers, such as the U.S. Navy SEALs, are trained to conduct underwater combat operations. These missions may include placing explosives, sabotaging enemy ships, infiltrating coastal areas, and other combat-related tasks. Combat divers are highly trained and can operate in low visibility, extreme temperatures, and strong currents.

- Explosive Ordnance Disposal (EOD): They are trained to detect, identify, and disarm underwater mines, improvised explosive devices (IEDs), and other types of munitions. These operations require advanced diving skills and high precision, as any mistake can be fatal. Most EOD teams use closed-circuit diving techniques to avoid detection while performing these sensitive missions.

- Ice diving: In Arctic or Antarctic environments, navy divers must dive in extreme cold conditions, which involves diving under ice. This type of diving requires additional skills due to extremely low temperatures, reduced visibility, and the lack of exit points. Divers are typically connected to the surface via lifelines to ensure their safety.

- Rescue and recovery operations: Navy divers are also trained in underwater rescues, such as rescuing submarines or crews trapped underwater. These operations often involve the use of rescue bells, hyperbaric chambers, and other specialized equipment to access great depths and rescue people from dangerous environments.

- Tunnel or confined space diving: Divers must be trained to navigate narrow, dark passages, often without the possibility of turning around or retreating. This can be extremely claustrophobic and dangerous.

Printed in Great Britain
by Amazon